SPECIAL OPERATIONS FORCES

Special Operations Forces:
Building Global Partnerships

EDITED BY:

Dr. Emily Spencer

CANADIAN DEFENCE ACADEMY PRESS

Canadian Defence Academy Press
PO Box 17000 Stn Forces
Kingston, Ontario   K7K 7B4

Produced for the Canadian Defence Academy Press
by 17 Wing Winnipeg Publishing Office.
WPO30804

Library and Archives Canada Cataloguing in Publication

Special operations forces : building global partnerships / edited by Emily Spencer.

Produced for the Canadian Defence Academy Press by 17 Wing Winnipeg Publishing Office.
Includes bibliographical references and index.
Available also on the Internet.
Issued by: Canadian Defence Academy.
Co-published by: CANSOFCOM Professional Development Centre.
ISBN 978-1-100-20763-6 (bound).--ISBN 978-1-100-20764-3 (pbk.)
Cat. no.: D2-303/1-2012E (bound)
Cat. no.: D2-303/2-2012E (pbk.)

1. Special forces (Military science)--Congresses.   2. Military assistance--Congresses.   3. Military education--Congresses.   I. Spencer, Emily   II. Canadian Defence Academy   III. Canada. Canadian Armed Forces. Wing, 17   IV. Canada. Canadian Special Operations Forces Command. Professional Development Centre

U262 S63 2012   356'.16   C2012-980122-4

Printed in Canada.

1 3 5 7 9 10 8 6 4 2

CANADIAN DEFENCE ACADEMY PRESS

TABLE OF CONTENTS

TABLE OF CONTENTS

FOREWORD

Special Operations Forces (SOF) are infinitely able to provide more than simply rapidly deployable, precise, kinetic force capability to any area in the world. In addition to this empowering skill set, SOF also bring a softer edge to the table. Comprised of members who are selected for their creativity, adaptability and ability to be agile thinkers among other things, SOF are an excellent match for Defence, Diplomacy and Military Assistance (DDMA) type missions or, to use the America lexicon, Foreign Internal Defense (FID)/Security Force Assistance (SFA). Notably, this type of capacity building requires individuals to simultaneously be scholars, diplomats and warriors as they train and work with host nation partner forces. Indeed, regardless of the specific terminology, these tasks are about building capacity and require a multitude of skill-sets to be executed effectively.

Essentially capacity building is about helping allies who possess the will but not necessarily the capacity or expertise to conduct counter-terrorism operations. As such, it is vital to our national interests for many reasons.

First, regional threats have a better chance of being contained within a region, or eliminated before they grow beyond the region if partner nations receive support in addressing the problem. To put it plainly, threats are eliminated before they reach our borders, or at least contained within remote and inhospitable areas where terrorists have a limited ability to pose a threat to others.

Second, transnational threats represent a common enemy, therefore, by cooperating with partner nations and building relationships, the global terror network is engaged by an equally robust or superior network. International military training assistance by its very nature serves to create the network of "good guys" that will defeat the network of "bad guys."

Third, by training others, we train ourselves. While some people erroneously view capacity building as a paternalistic undertaking, this perspective is severely limited. Many partners may need our assistance in certain areas, but they have much to offer in others. For example, we may have the technology, whereas they may possess the cultural understanding to secure the trust of local populations. Additionally, they may be more expert on a given type of terrain or more capable of withstanding climactic conditions such as extreme heat or cold, or perhaps they have been making do with very little for very long and possess a resourcefulness that we can all respect and learn from.

Finally, we cannot ignore the current global economic situation. The Canadian and US governments, as well as most European nations, have declared war on deficits and, rightfully, are committed to improving economic conditions in both a national and international context.

As such, the *SOF: Building Global Partnerships* symposium held at the Royal Military College of Canada, 5-7 December 2011, was an important step in opening this dialogue from the academic, military, governmental and civilian perspectives, among others. This volume represents an amalgam of the presentations and ideas that were put forward by scholars and military practitioners in order to both educate, as well as create discourse on the subject of SOF, particularly with respect to DDMA type missions.

Notably, for the first time this symposium was co-sponsored by the US Joint Special Operations University, as well as the Royal Military College of Canada (RMCC) and the Canadian Special Operations Forces Command. It is with great pleasure that we welcome our American colleagues as we eagerly learn from each other's experiences.

Accordingly, it is with great pleasure that I introduce this collection of essays that explore the less kinetic, but no less valuable, contributions that SOF make to the contemporary operating environment. As our Command motto, *Viam Inveniemus*, states, we will find a way.

D.W. Thompson
Brigadier-General
Commander
Canadian Special Operations Forces Command

INTRODUCTION

Often the mystique of special operations forces overshadows the reality of this group of specially selected, trained and employed individuals. The Hollywood image of SOF is generally that of a muscular male armed to the teeth who saves the world with his physical prowess and quick trigger finger. The truth, however, is much more refined and complex. In the end, SOF perform a variety of tasks, both kinetic and non-kinetic, in order to further national interests at home and abroad.

SOF: Building Global Partnerships explores some of the ways in which SOF are employed in a largely non-kinetic manner, particularly in their role of providing military assistance and training to foreign militaries. As one can imagine, there are many tasks that fall under this rubric as SOF work, often alongside other governmental organizations and agencies as well as non-governmental organizations, to help provide foreign militaries with a well-trained SOF capability of their own.

Originating with the formulation of national foreign policy initiatives and extending down to the individual operator, it is not surprising that building global partnerships through military assistance and training is a complicated process. Moreover, each level encounters its own set of challenges and rewards.

As such, *SOF: Building Global Partnerships* is organized in such a way as to first layout some of the issues at the national policy level, then to identify through personal accounts some of the challenges of training others. The volume then closes with some prescriptive guidelines for effectively working with foreign militaries. While no single volume could do justice to the topic at hand, *SOF: Building Global Partnerships* provides a good base for understanding the complexity of the issue of working with international partners.

This volume is largely derived from presentations and topics that were explored during the SOF Symposium held at the Royal Military College of Canada from 5-7 December 2011. Notably, this Symposium marked the first time that the US Joint Special Operations University joined the RMCC and the Canadian Special Operations Forces Command (CANSOFCOM) in co-hosting the event. We warmly toast our new partnership as we look forward to many more co-hosted symposia.

CHAPTER 1

FORCE OF CHOICE:
SOF AS A FOREIGN POLICY ENABLER

COLONEL BERND HORN, PhD
AND DR. EMILY SPENCER

The Canadian economy relies on international trade and for this reason, as well as perhaps a more altruistic, yet connected, commitment to global peace and stability, the Government of Canada (GoC) can ill afford to have an isolationist stance. As such, a strong foreign policy is the cornerstone to a well functioning government. Indeed, during the past century, the GoC has for the most part adhered to this principle. For example, Canada has participated in major global conflicts such as the two world wars of the 20th century, and the Korean War, joined key international bodies and alliances such as the United Nations (UN) and the North Atlantic Treaty Organization (NATO), and participated in major peace support operations throughout the post-Second World War era, and more recently committed troops to Afghanistan.

The GoC's commitment to a strong foreign policy is enabled by many key federal departments and agencies. While there is no question that the execution of foreign policy demands the cooperation and commitment of multiple departments and agencies, one of the key players is the Department of National Defence (DND). In particular, DND's global deployment of the Canadian Forces (CF) represents the most visceral commitment of "blood and treasure". As such, DND and the CF are key enablers of Canadian foreign policy.

Within the realm of the military, special operations forces are a key enabler. In particular, Canadian Special Operations Forces

1

(CANSOF) with their specialized and unique attributes and capabilities provide the GoC with a flexibility of options, both overt and covert. In the end, CANSOF with its small footprint, large repertoire of capabilities and skills, as well as its global reach, can become a force of choice, particularly, in this era of fiscal restraint yet increasing global instability.

WHY IS FOREIGN POLICY IMPORTANT?

Prior to delving into why and how SOF are the force of choice, it is first important to appreciate why foreign policy is crucial to domestic well-being and what exactly foreign policy entails. The requirement to engage in international affairs is often seen as assisting friends and allies and paying "dues" as an advanced Western democracy. However, much of what drives foreign policy is the hard edge of Carl von Clausewitz's "realpolitik." Canada's actions internationally have real economic, political and security consequences. Whether attempting to establish, or shore up, trade relations or economic agreements, or to ensure a seat at the table of an international body in order to be able to influence and shape international decisions or perspectives, or simply to protect Canadians and Canadian national interest, our engagement with the world is key.

It is also very pragmatic and at times self-serving. One need only look at recent events to realize that this statement is true. Canada's failure to get a seat on the UN Security Council in 2010 was a failure many critics claimed was the result of the government's inability to create a coherent foreign policy that adequately engaged its international partners. The consequence of this shortsightedness was seemingly dramatic and swift. In a different context, a former commander of Canadian Expeditionary Force Command (CEFCOM) commented "we went to Afghanistan to atone for our sins in Iraq" referring to American anger at the Canadian government's refusal to participate in its 2003 invasion of Iraq.

Indeed, relations between the US and Canadian governments, as well as their militaries, were strained during this period. Political and economic issues such as mad cow disease, softwood lumber, pacific salmon and border security dominated the headlines as the Americans took a hard-line stance. However, in 2005, once Canada committed ground troops to combat in southern Afghanistan, the contentious issues seemingly disappeared.[1] Certainly one would have to be naïve to believe that that the issues were not at all related. More arguable is the assumption that there is always a countervailing force to acts of omission or commission in international relations. They are not always overtly stated but the subtext, nuance and coincidence of unfavourable decisions or actions by others is normally clear.

The fact that globalization and a turbulent contemporary global security environment impact all nations is an example of another pragmatic reality that is accounted for during decision-making. A government report noted:

> *The world is changing, quickly and radically, and these changes matter to Canada – not in abstract terms, and not only to students of international relations, but tangibly and to everyone. Our security, our prosperity and our quality of life all stand to be influenced and affected by these global transformations and by the challenges they bring – from the spectre of international terrorism to the threats of virulent disease, climate change and disappearing fish stocks. It is through our foreign policy that Canada must and will act to ensure that we as a nation overcome the trials and embrace the opportunities of the 21st Century.[2]*

Along a similar vein, a former minister of the Department of Foreign Affairs and International Trade (DFAIT) insisted, "Canadians have an increasing stake in international developments. The food we eat, the air we breathe, and our health, safety, prosperity and quality of life are increasingly affected by what happens beyond our borders."[3] This sentiment was echoed by the *Canada First Defence Strategy* (CFDS) issued in June 2008. It noted, "Globalization means that developments abroad can have a profound impact on the safety and interests of Canadians at home."[4]

Moreover, there is also the question of security. As former Chief of the Defence Staff General Rick Hillier asserted, "the best defence for Canada is a good offence (i.e. assist with global security and combat instability elsewhere)." He explained, "We must play a significant part in the world to prevent that violence and conflict from coming home."[5] More recently in February 2012, Peter MacKay, the Minister of National Defence (MND), while at Stanford University in California, presented that "domestic security issues begin internationally and it's best to act before they happen." The logic of Hillier and MacKay's reasoning is sound. It is also in consonance with DFAIT policy, which asserts that "a world that is peaceful and prosperous, in which democracy and respect for human rights flourish, is a world of opportunity for Canada and for Canadians."[6]

Importantly, this reasoning appears to resonate with Canadians. A recent study concluded that "despite the stereotypes of the pacifist Canadian public and the belligerent Americans, Canadians are very similar to Americans in our willingness to commit the military." The study continued to note that "it appears the main difference between Americans and Canadians when it comes to committing troops is not Canadian commitment but Canadian capability."[7] The report concluded that "Canadians are overwhelmingly ready to commit troops."[8] In sum, the study found that Canadians "are strongly oriented toward taking an active role on the world stage." It noted that "Canada is a country that firmly believes it has played a major role in the significant world events of the past 75 years. While there is no consensus among the general public on whether Canada is becoming stronger or weaker internationally, those who are most concerned believe we are losing ground in terms of our influence."[9] Importantly, the report emphasized that "three quarters of Canadians reject the idea that 'What happens in the rest of the world really doesn't make much of a difference to me in my daily life.' Half the country strongly rejects that premise."[10]

The message is certainly that if you want to influence the game, you must be a player. Regardless of whether you want to increase economic prosperity through trade, gain a "seat at the table" and have some influence in shaping international events or international response to events, or if you are concerned with protecting sovereignty, citizens or Canadian interest, or any combination there of, in the end, you must be a player. As a nation, you must engage internationally, and you must contribute national blood and treasure towards both the organizations that shape international response to crisis, as well as the response itself. How the nation engages in this process is in the simplest of terms through its foreign policy.

Within a nation's foreign policy, the military becomes a key component of or, if you will, government tool to help implement, foreign policy. The military is arguably the most overt of mechanisms that a country can use to demonstrate its willingness to participate in international events. It is certainly the tool that best demonstrates its commitment to such endeavours. After all, economic incentives/embargoes/contributions, while effective on different economic, political and social levels, do not signal intent, importance, or commitment to the same degree as military "boots on the ground." Military action is the most dramatic, rapid, entwining and overt message to the international stage that an issue is of significant importance to the player(s) involved.

BUT WHAT EXACTLY IS FOREIGN POLICY?

As a senate committee clearly articulated, "Foreign Policy is made, it is not given. It is the continual process of exercising political will and of mobilizing national resources to meet international challenges and address national interest."[11] A former

Prime Minister explained, "foreign policy is how a nation best expresses itself to the world. Our policies as a government, reflecting our beliefs as Canadians, are articulated through the words we speak, the decisions we make and the actions we implement in the name of Canada."[12] Similarly, Pierre Pettigrew, a former Minister of Foreign Affairs, believed that foreign policy is "an outward expression of our society."[13]

Foreign policy is significantly shaped by international forces. For instance, alliances, coalition partners, trading partners, international considerations and events all impact on a nation's foreign policy. Decisions taken have, as already noted, consequences, both positive and negative.

Internal domestic dynamics also impact foreign policy. After all, domestic issues affect Canadians in their daily lives, ranging from their standard of living, employment, the environment, the management of resources, the question of refugees seeking asylum, as well as friends and loved ones being put in harm's way in conflicts abroad. Arguably, a nation's foreign policy impacts a nation's prosperity, quality of life and security. As such, domestic issues are taken into strong consideration when developing foreign policy.

This relationship is clearly evident when one considers that Canada is a trading nation. In fact, Canada is the world's fifth largest exporter and importer. Trade "is equivalent to more than 70% of our gross domestic product (GDP). Exports account for almost 40 percent of the Canadian economy and are linked to one-quarter of all Canadian jobs."[14] As such, how we engage in, and with, the world is directly related to prosperity, quality of life and security at home.

In short, isolationism or a weak and unsubstantiated foreign policy is not an option. Canada must remain engaged internationally, especially with such organizations as the G8, G20, UN, NATO,

Asia-Pacific Economic Cooperation (APEC), Gulf Co-operation Council (GCC) and the Association of Southeast Asian Nations (ASEAN). Moreover, Canada must participate, influence and shape others around the table to ensure Canadian concerns, needs and interests are, at a minimum, considered in decision-making and subsequent actions.

Throughout the Cold War (c.1948-1989) Canada maintained a consistent theme in its foreign policy. It was based on a reliance on alliances (i.e. the US, UK, NATO and engagement in the UN) while advancing long-standing core Canadian values that have always been cornerstones of Canada's foreign policy, namely the rule of law, democratic rights and freedoms, respect for the dignity of others and human rights.

Within this framework, congruence between foreign and defence policies was always very high.[15] However, this correspondence has not always been the case in the post-Cold War era and continues to shift as Canada looked to, and continues to pursue engagement with, non-traditional trading partners, countries and regions. This present day situation is representative of an evolving Canadian international outlook and foreign policy.

How the country engages others internationally, as already discussed, is normally captured in the nation's foreign policy, which often takes the form of a "White Paper." The last official foreign policy White Paper was the 1995 release of *Canada in the World.* Although dated, the document does provide insight into Canadian foreign policy and has been augmented by continual updates in the form of departmental policy statements.

Nonetheless, many of the core concepts captured in *Canada in the World* remain valid to this day. The 1995 White Paper explained that Canada's position in the world is to "influence change and to benefit from opportunities." It also stated that the government would "exercise that influence and responsibility to protect and to promote Canada's values and interests in the world." It included three key objectives:

    a. promotion of prosperity;

    b. protection of our security within a global framework; and

    c. projection of Canadian values and culture.[16]

An underlying tenet of the White Paper was a recognition that Canada be increasingly reliant on a fundamental interdependence with the rest of the world that was rooted in economic and trade between countries and regions. This tenet was further reinforced in the series of 2005 DFAIT policy directives. Moreover, more recent policy directives also emphasized the importance of international security. As illustrated, the government has continually underlined the importance of ensuring a stable and secure international security environment through partnerships.

Keeping in mind the factors noted, the current government continues to evolve its foreign policy.[17] In order to accomplish its goals, the Canadian Government has identified more than a dozen priority countries, China being among them.[18] Apparently, a new foreign policy plan is imminent. In the interim DFAIT has identified key priorities:

    a. Priority #1: Greater economic opportunity for Canada, with a focus on growing/emerging markets;

    b. Priority #2: United States and the Americas;

    c. Priority #3: Afghanistan, including in the context of neighbouring countries;

    d. Priority #4: Asserting Canadian leadership in emerging global governance; and

    e. Priority #5: Transforming the department.[19]

These priorities will inform and shape the national foreign policy until such time as a new governmental White Paper or policy statement(s) is drafted. The direction in whatever form it exists will also be critical in providing direction for other government departments in their international engagements and commitments. Notably, as mentioned, DND is a key player in helping to execute foreign policy.

DND / CF AND FOREIGN POLICY

The role of the military in enabling foreign policy is intuitively clear. Former Minister of National Defence Bill Graham insisted that "the government recognizes that the Canadian Forces are a vital instrument of Canada's foreign policy, especially in today's unstable world."[20] This view was reinforced by Peter Mackay during the release of the current Defence White Paper, the *Canada First Defence Strategy* in June 2008. He re-asserted the CF's requirement to "support the Government's broader national security and foreign policy objectives by maintaining the ability to deliver excellence at home, be a strong and reliable partner in the defence of North America, and project leadership abroad by making meaningful contributions to operations overseas."[21]

Importantly, Prime Minister Stephen Harper, in his introduction of the CFDS, began by underlining the importance of the military with regard to international relations and Canadian status abroad. He declared:

> *This Government took office with a firm commitment to stand up for Canada. Fulfilling this obligation means keeping our citizens safe and secure, defending our sovereignty, and ensuring that Canada can return to the international stage as a credible and influential country ready to do its part.*[22]

These statements underscore the military as a key component of foreign policy.

Notably, the nexus between defence policy and foreign policy is the national security policy. The national security policy is the filter through which foreign policy informs defence policy. It contributes to the larger foreign policy agenda by providing national "interests" and priorities. In essence, it places peace and security issues into the foreign policy context while devolving onto defence policy the obligations and commitments, including the development of doctrine and procedures and the ensuing allocation of scarce resources, appropriate to ensuring that Canada's military commitments are sustainable and credible.[23]

The government has given DND, through its CFDS and policy statements, the task "to provide combat-capable, multi-purpose forces for employment both at home and abroad to protect Canada and Canadians, and to deliver strategic effect for Canada."[24] Moreover, it has set out three key roles:

a. Defend Canada;

b. Defend North America; and

c. Contribute to international peace and security.[25]

In line with the 2008 CFDS, the government assigned DND six core missions:

a. Conduct daily domestic and continental operations, including in the Arctic and through NORAD [North American Aerospace Defence Command];

b. Support a major international event in Canada such as the G8, G20;

c. Respond to a major terrorist attack;

d. Support civilian authorities during a crisis in Canada such as a natural disaster;

e. Lead and/or conduct a major international operation for an extended period; and

f. Deploy forces in response to crises elsewhere in the world for shorter periods.[26]

The net effect of DND/CF's efforts is captured in the four strategic outcomes that are embedded in the expectations of the government and people of Canada. Quite simply they anticipate that:

a. Defence operations will improve peace, stability and security wherever deployed;

b. National Defence is ready to meet Government defence expectations;

c. Resources are acquired to meet Government defence expectations; and

d. Care and support to the CF and contribution to Canadian society.[27]

An examination of the roles, tasks and outcomes clearly demonstrates the strong and influential role the military plays in executing foreign policy. Moreover, this role becomes even more impressive when one considers that the tasks assigned are not necessarily weighted accordingly in execution. For example, although the defence of Canada is clearly the CF's number one priority that does not mean that it is the emphasis or focus of activity on a "day-to-day" basis. It comes down to a question of risk and what other priorities are facing the country and the government. For example, during Canada's combat role in Afghanistan (c. 2006-2011), the focus of DND/CF, and particularly the Army, was supporting its warfighting efforts in Afghanistan. Clearly, direct threats to Canada were extremely low during this period, whereas the risk in Afghanistan to our service personnel, our obligations to our allies and coalition partners, and our commitment to improving the governance, development and security of Afghanistan, were relatively high. As such, the requirement to contribute to international peace and security took on a much greater prominence than the other roles on a day-to-day basis.

It is without doubt that the emphasis on assisting international security as part of the DND/CF foreign policy contribution is significant. In 2011-2012, the government assigned DND a total budget of $21,299,079,000.00. In turn, DND allocated $3,146,676,000.00 for operations to improve peace, stability and security.[28] When one considers that approximately half of the budget is consumed by personnel expenditures, the proportionate weight placed on support to foreign policy initiatives becomes clearer.

However, that is only part of the picture. The military also advances foreign policy through the mechanism of defence diplomacy, which includes such activities as high-level visits, international personnel placements, Canadian Defence Attachés, training and capacity building, joint exercises and legal, technical and logistical arrangements. These activities are coordinated and implemented through a Global Engagement Strategy. Lieutenant-General Walter Semianiw, a former commander of Canada Command, stated, "The global engagement strategy clearly lays out the priority of support to different countries."[29] In concert with Government of Canada direction, and in coordination with DFAIT, each year DND, through Associate Deputy Minister – Policy (ADM–POL), generates a Military Training and Cooperation Program (MTCP) Regional and Country Policy Priorities list.[30] ADM–POL, through MTCP, chairs a Military Assistance Steering Committee (MASC), which in turn provides input at an annual review process establishing regional and country priorities in line with government direction. This policy then determines: where CF training and advisory teams will deploy; where joint exercises may be conducted; where defence education outreach will be targeted; and where CF students may attend courses or staff college and where invitations for foreign students to attend Canadian courses and staff college (as well as how many) will be allocated. As such, the military becomes an essential instrument in executing foreign policy and developing opportunities and events to establish, build and nurture partnerships and relationships.

In the end, the military is arguably one of the most important instruments of applying national foreign policy. It provides the mechanism to assist with providing aid, military training assistance and advice, governance, development, and security, particularly in regions in the world where conflict and lawlessness is rampant and normal foreign aid and developmental models cannot work. Undisputedly, the deployment of the military, specifically "boots on the ground," is the most powerful and graphic symbol of national will and commitment.[31] After all, once a nation commits its military to an operation, it has clearly shown that it has committed its "blood and treasure." This type of commitment has dramatic domestic implications, as it does international consequences.[32]

As such, military engagement is a currency of international affairs. To sit at the table and have a voice to influence and shape world events, a nation, specifically an advanced Western democracy, needs to pay "dues." Canada's voice in NATO and the UN, for instance, is vested in its ability and willingness to share in the "heavy lifting" of providing troops for international security operations. It is difficult to have a say, or to complain of one's lack of voice and influence, when one sits on the sidelines and lets others take the risk and cover the cost of military action.

SOF & FOREIGN POLICY

Within the military inventory of tools to achieve necessary effect, SOF offer a wide range of capabilities and options that, arguably, make them the force of choice as a foreign policy enabler. Prior to articulating SOF's important contribution to foreign policy, it is important to clearly define what they are. In essence, "Special

Operation Forces are organizations containing specially selected personnel that are organized, equipped and trained to conduct high-risk, high value special operations to achieve military, political, economic or informational objectives by using special and unique operational methodologies in hostile, denied or politically sensitive areas to achieve desired tactical, operational and/or strategic effects in times of peace, conflict or war."[33]

A key factor to SOF success, and why they are so effective in contributing to foreign policy, is in fact due to its personnel. Individuals who are attracted to SOF, who volunteer and who are ultimately chosen to serve in SOF as a result of highly refined selection procedures and standards, are what provide the catalyst for mission success. Quite simply, SOF organizations seek individuals who are:

1. Risk accepting – individuals who are not reckless, but rather carefully consider all options and consequences and balance the risk of acting versus the failure to act. They possess the moral courage to make decisions and take action within the commander's intent and their legal parameters of action to achieve mission success;

2. Creative – individuals who are capable of assessing a situation and deriving innovative solutions, kinetic or non-kinetic, to best resolve a particular circumstance. In essence, they have the intellectual and experiential ability to immediately change the combat process;

3. Agile Thinkers – individuals who are able to transition between tasks quickly and effortlessly. They can perform multiple tasks at the same time, in the same place with the same forces. They can seamlessly transition from kinetic to non-kinetic or vice versa employing the entire spectrum of military, political, social and economic solutions to complex problems to achieve the desired outcomes.

They can react quickly to rapidly changing situations and transition between widely different activities and ensure they position themselves to exploit fleeting opportunities. Moreover, they can work effectively within rules of engagement (ROE) in volatile, ambiguous and complex threat environments and use the appropriate levels of force;

4. Adaptive – individuals who respond effectively to changing situations and tasks as they arise. They do not fear the unknown and embrace change as an inherent and important, dynamic element in the evolution of organizations, warfare and society;

5. Self-Reliant – individuals who exercise professional military judgment and disciplined initiative to achieve the commander's intent without the necessity of constant supervision, support or encouragement. They accept that neither rank, nor appointment solely define responsibility for mission success. They function cohesively as part of a team but also perform superbly as individuals. They continue to carry on with a task until it becomes impossible to do so. They take control of their own professional development, personal affairs and destiny, and ensure they strive to become the best possible military professional achievable. They demonstrate constant dedication, initiative and discipline and maintain the highest standards of personal conduct. They understand that they are responsible and accountable for their actions at all times and always make the correct moral decisions regardless of situation or circumstance;

6. Eager for Challenge – individuals who have an unconquerable desire to fight and win. They have an unflinching acceptance of risk and a mindset that accepts that no challenge is too great. They are tenacious, unyielding and unremitting in the pursuit of mission success;

7. Naturally Orientated to the Pursuit of Excellence – individuals who consistently demonstrate an uncompromising, persistent effort to excel at absolutely everything they do. Their driving focus is to attain the highest standards of personal, professional and technical expertise, competence and integrity. They have an unremitting emphasis on continually adapting, innovating and learning to achieve the highest possible standards of personal, tactical and operational proficiency and effectiveness;

8. Relentless in their pursuit of Mission Success – Individuals who embody a belief that first and foremost is service to country before self. They have an unwavering dedication to mission success and an acceptance of hardship and sacrifice. They strive to achieve mission success at all costs, yet within full compliance of legal mandates, civil law and the law of armed conflict; and

9. Culturally Attuned – Individuals who are warrior-diplomats, who are comfortable fighting but equally skilled at finding non-kinetic solutions to problems. They are capable of operating individually, in small teams or larger organizations integrally, or with allies and coalition partners. They are also comfortable and adept at dealing with civilians, other government departments (OGD) and international organizations, as well as non-governmental organizations (NGOs). They are culturally attuned and understand that it is important to "see reality" through the eyes of another culture. They understand that it is not the message that was intended that is important but rather the message that was received that matters. They strive to be empathetic, understanding and respectful at all times when dealing with others. They comprehend that respect and understanding build trust, credibility and mission success.[34]

As a result, SOF have personnel who bring superb skill, knowledge, experience and cognitive agility to any task. Therefore, armed with exceptional individuals, as well as cutting edge technology and equipment, SOF offer the government a wide range of capability that can meet its specific foreign policy requirements. For example, Defence, Diplomacy, and Military Assistance is an important mission set that falls under the rubric of high value tasks (HVTs) and refers to "operations that contribute to nation building through assistance to select states through the provision of specialized military advice, training and assistance."[35] Within DND, SOF are particularly suited to fulfill this mandate because of the skill-sets and attributes SOF personnel possess. Their technical proficiency and skills, as well as their intellectual agility provide them with the ability to operate in alien, ambiguous, complex and ever changing environments. These qualities also reflect the often unique ability of SOF to interact effectively with indigenous forces and populations in order to achieve government objectives and goals.

The governmental nexus is an important component of DDMA since the missions are designed to achieve effects that can serve the national interest. These effects include providing the Canadian Government with:

1. Assistance to partner nations as part of our foreign policy global engagement;

2. Assistance to partner nations in increasing their ability to stabilize the security of their homeland. Importantly, by participating in increasing global stability offshore, we indirectly protect Canada by stemming the flow of such negative effects originating from the consequences of organized crime, terrorism, and instability that creates humanitarian and refugee issues;

3. An ability to help shape the global response to international terrorism and thereby helping to ensure that all states are able to cope with, and respond to, the growing web of international terrorism and organized crime which assists with limiting the global reach of those organizations;

4. The provision of ground truth and situational awareness based on accurate unbiased reporting that helps to provide the necessary information to make the necessary informed policy decisions;

5. The creation of "virtual forward operating bases (FOBs)" that can be used in emergencies to extend global reach or assist our partners. Additionally, these "virtual" forward operating bases become crucial for a resource constrained and small military force such as the CF. These networks of countries provide Canada with partners who are known to one another (i.e. in training; doctrine; tactics, techniques and procedures (TTPs), and standard operating procedures (SOPs)) and thus allow for increased options potentially open to the Government of Canada in a crisis;

6. A network of interoperable partner nations capable of working together in a regional context to provide security and stability;

7. The provision of regional experience and exposure, as well as the development of personal networks for operators and SOF personnel writ large; and

8. The personal development of SOF operators as culturally savvy trainers and educators who can operate adeptly in foreign and alien cultures.

However, DDMA aside, SOF also offer the government a wide array of other non-kinetic, as well as kinetic, options to preempt, disrupt, react or shape operational or strategic effects internationally or within a specific theatre.[36] Simply put, SOF provide a number of options and a wide range of capabilities not always resident in conventional forces. Specifically they can:

1. Conduct surgical precision operations with lethal or non-lethal effects;

2. Rapidly deploy specially configured SOF task forces that tailor organizational design and force structure to meet the specific need of a mission or task;

3. Operate seamlessly in combined, joint, or integrated environments or force structures;

4. Infiltrate and extract from hostile or denied areas, and operate within those designated areas in an overt or clandestine manner;

5. Survive and operate in a variety of harsh and hostile environments for extended periods of time;

6. Operate in a self-sufficient manner for extended periods of time;

7. Bring expertise and influence to an area due to their level of cultural awareness, training and operational methodologies; and

8. Bring a dominance in command, control, communications, computers, intelligence, surveillance and reconnaissance (C4ISR) to the operational area providing informational superiority, which in turn allows for rapid decisive action that can shape an area of operation (AO).

In addition, SOF underscore their status as a key foreign policy enabler for the government because of its unrivalled capability combined with its global reach, specifically, SOF's ability to rapidly deploy and operate anywhere on the globe, from the formidable Arctic regions in the North, to the inhospitable jungles of Africa, to the harsh deserts of North Africa and southwest Asia. SOF capability translates into equipped, trained, organized and rapidly deployed forces capable of operating in all environments and climates. Furthermore, SOF is networked and interoperable with its key allies and able to operate independently or within a joint, integrated or coalition framework. Finally, SOF is enabled with the necessary resources (e.g. lift; Intelligence, Surveillance and Reconnaissance (ISR); air effects) to conduct operations with the minimum amount of external support. It is also able to leverage cultural agility through its ability to operate effectively in many disparate operational environments, and through and with a broad selection of host nations.

As such, SOF provide a self-contained, versatile and unique range of capabilities, whether employed alone or complementing other forces or agencies to attain governmental foreign policy effects. In contrast to conventional forces, SOF are generally small, precise, adaptable and innovative. They can conduct operations in a clandestine, covert or discreet manner.[37] They are capable of organizing and deploying rapidly and can gain entry to and operate in hostile or denied areas without the necessity of secured ports, airfields or road networks. Importantly, they can operate in normal diplomatic, training or exercise environments, as well as in austere and harsh environments. Moreover, they can communicate worldwide with integral equipment.

In sum, SOF provide the government with agile, robust, high-readiness forces that are organized, equipped and trained to conduct high-risk, high-value special operations across the spectrum of conflict at home and abroad to achieve military, political, economic or informational objectives in defence of the country or the national interest in hostile, denied or politically sensitive areas in times of peace, conflict or war. Therefore, CANSOF with its small footprint, large repertoire of capabilities and skills, as well as its global reach, should be the force of choice in this era of fiscal restraint yet increasing global instability. For a trading nation such as Canada, a strong foreign policy is crucial to a prosperous and stable domestic situation. The CF is instrumental in ensuring that this is the case and increasingly SOF will play a vital role in this process.

NOTES

1   What is important to the Americans and what they think, whether Canadians like it or not, are also important to us. In 2005 terms, Canada and the United States exchanged $1.8 billion in goods and services every day of the year – well over $1 million a minute. By 2012, this increased to over $2 billion daily. See Canada, *"Introduction," Canada's International Policy Statement. A Role of Pride and Influence in the World – Commerce* (Ottawa: DFAIT, 2005), 2; and Department of Foreign Affairs and International Trade, "Minister's Message," <http://www.tbs-sct.gc.ca/rpp/2010-2011/inst/ext/ext01-eng.asp#s11>, accessed 28 December 2011.

2   Paul Martin, "Foreword from the Prime Minister," *Canada's International Policy Statement. A Role of Pride and Influence in the World - Overview* (Ottawa: DFAIT, 2005), i.

3   Pierre Pettigrew, "Message From the Minister," *Canada's International Policy Statement. A Role of Pride and Influence in the World - Diplomacy* (Ottawa: DFAIT, 2005), 1.

4   Canada, *Canada First Defence Strategy* (Ottawa: DND, 2008), 6.

5   Lieutenant-General Rick Hillier, Chief of the Land Staff (CLS) address to Army Strategic Planning Session 7, 29 November 2003, Cornwall Ontario.

6   Pettigrew, 1.

7   Innovative Research Group, Inc., "Visions of Canadian Foreign Policy. Conference Report," *Canadian Defence & Foreign Affairs Institute*, 4 November 2004, 5.

8   The article continued to break this support down by category noting that "even the least popular reason for committing troops – securing the supply of oil enjoys more support (47%) than opposition (45%)." Assisting a population struck by famine was supported by 92 percent of Canadians; upholding international law was supported by 84 percent (and strongly supported by 55 percent); bringing peace in a civil war 79 percent; to liberate hostages by 78 percent (and strongly supported by 49 percent); and to destroy a terrorist camp by 73 percent of Canadians. Ibid., 4.

9   Ibid., 4.

10   Ibid., 26.

11   Allan J. MacEachen and Jean-Robert Gauthier, *Canada's Foreign Policy: Principles and Priorities for the Future. Report of the Special Joint Committee of the Senate and the House of Commons Reviewing Canadian Foreign Policy*, November 1994, 3-6.

12   Martin, i.

13   Pettigrew, i.

14   See Canada, "*Introduction*," C*anada's International Policy Statement. A Role of Pride and Influence in the World - Commerce* (Ottawa: DFAIT, 2005), 1; and Paul Heinbecker, "Human Security: The Hard Edge," *Canadian Military Journal*, Vol 1, No. 1 (Spring 2000), 12.

15   See Report of the Standing Senate Committee on Foreign Affairs, *Meeting New Challenge: Canada's Response to a New Generation of Peacekeeping*, February 1993, 2. During the Cold War, Canada's participation in NATO arguably drove its foreign policy. This led former Prime Minister Pierre Trudeau to rail, "It is a false perspective to have a military alliance determine your foreign policy. It should be your foreign policy which determines your military policy." Cited in D.W. Middlemiss and

J.J. Sokolsky, *Canadian Defence. Decisions and Determinants* (Toronto: Harcourt Brace Jovanovich, 1993), 6.

16   See Canada, *Canada in the World* (Ottawa: DFAIT, 1995).

17   The official DFAIT website explains its role as promoting Canada's interests and the security and prosperity of Canadians. It also explains that it advances the Canadian values of democracy, human rights, the rule of law and environmental stewardship. These have largely remained constant throughout the Cold War and post-Cold War era.

18   Apparently, in addition to China, priority countries include: India, Indonesia, Mexico, Brazil, Turkey, North Korea and South Africa.

19   Department of Foreign Affairs and International Trade, "Minister's Message," <http://www.tbs-sct.gc.ca/rpp/2010-2011/inst/ext/ext01-eng.asp#s11>, accessed 28 December 2011.

20   Bill Graham, *"Message From the Minister,"* *Canada's International Policy Statement. A Role of Pride and Influence in the World – Defence* (Ottawa: DND, 2005), i.

21   Canada, *CFDS*, 2.

22   Ibid., 1.

23   See David B. Dewitt and David Leyton-Brown eds., *Canada's International Security Policy* (Scarborough, ON: Prentice Hall, 1995), 1-28 for a more fulsome discussion of national security policy.

24   Canada. *Report on Plans and Priorities 2011-2012 Part III - Estimates* (Ottawa: DND, 2011), 6.

25   Canada, *CFDS*, 7; and Canada. *Report on Plans and Priorities 2011-2012 Part III - Estimates*, 6. The defence objectives (DO) have remained largely unchanged. They are:

      a.   DO 1 – to provide strategic defence and security advice to the government;

b. DO 2 — to conduct surveillance and control of Canada's territory, aerospace and maritime areas of jurisdiction;

c. DO 3 — to respond to requests for Aid to the Civil Power;

d. DO 4 — to participate in bilateral and multilateral operations

e. DO 5 — to assist other government departments and other levels of government in achieving national goals;

f. DO 6 — to provide support to broad government programs;

g. DO 7 — to provide emergency and humanitarian relief; and

h. DO 8 — to maximize defence capabilities through the efficient and effective use of resources.

Canada, *Defence Planning Guidance 2001* (Ottawa: DND, 2000), para 204.

26   Canada, *CFDS*, 10; and Canada, *Report on Plans and Priorities 2011-2012 Part III - Estimates*, 8. The impact of CF operations on, as well as the influence of, Canadian foreign policy is evident in the CF civil military relations (CMR) objectives on operations. They are to:

a. support Canadian national interests;

b. fulfill obligations imposed by domestic and international law, the four Geneva Conventions and the two Additional Protocols of 1977, and treaties and memoranda of understanding and agreements;

c. advise, assist or reinforce foreign governments in accordance with national policy and operational requirements;

d. support the Task Force's mission;

e. support specific Canadian politico-military objectives in theatre or Area of Operation;

f. assist Task Force in support of civil administration, in achieving developmental goals by assisting or reinforcing the judicial, executive and legislative branches of government, as well as political and socio-economic infrastructure to increase the effectiveness and efficiency of public institutions and civil services;

g. facilitate the [Task Force] TF mission of minimizing interference by the local population in the military phase of an operation while obtaining civil support for the civil phase and associated tasks;

h. assist the TF in meeting legal and moral obligations to the local population;

i. assist all commanders by providing those resources necessary to meet essential civil requirements, avoiding damage to civil property and usable resources, and minimizing loss of life and human suffering;

j. identify and coordinate the use of local resources, facilities and support such as civilian labour, transportation, communications, maintenance, medical facilities and supplies to restore local government;

k. support, as required, International Organizations (IOs), NGOs, the UN and OSCE, as well as NATO or national civilian agencies, in all types of civil-military cooperation and Peace Support Operations; and

l. assist Canadian and foreign civil authorities in creating, restoring and maintaining public law and order.

27 Canada. *Report on Plans and Priorities 2011-2012 Part III - Estimates*, 7.

28 Ibid., 12.

29 Chris Thatcher, "Expanded Horizons," *Vanguard*, October/November 2011, 11.

30 As the 2010-2011 *Directorate of Military Training and Cooperation (DMTC) Annual Report* notes, DMTC is "often DND's initial or only formal contact in many developing regions around the word." It administers the Military Training and Cooperation Program and special domestic and international projects both of which are "vital instruments in advancing Canada's defence diplomacy since they develop and enhance bilateral defence relationships with countries of strategic interest to Canada." 2010-2011 *Directorate of Military Training and Cooperation Annual Report*, 3.

31 "Boots on the ground" realistically means ground forces. Although air and naval forces are instrumental in complex, contemporary operations they do not symbolize the same degree of commitment. The fact is, once troops are committed to the ground it becomes difficult to extract

them, particularly once one has suffered casualties. It quickly becomes domestically a question of breaking faith with those who have fallen and inviting criticism as to why engagement was undertaken in the first place if the cause is so easily abandoned. From the international perspective withdrawal opens the nation up to lasting impressions of unreliability, a lack of national strength and will, a propensity to leave one's allies and coalition partners in the lurch and a failure to honour commitments made to both friends, allies, international organizations and needy countries. A large part of the difficulty of withdrawing forces stems from the reality of today's complex and media saturated security environment. Aircraft and naval ships are normally distant from the actual drama captured on the ground by journalists. It is the human drama of emotion, fear, death and tragedy that captures media sound bites. This is delivered in spades by troops on the ground fighting insurgents or dealing with host nation nationals who are caught in the grip of conflict. Aircraft high up in the sky or ships far out to sea cannot deliver this type of visual effect. Interviewing pilots on a hanger line or sea personnel on their immaculately clean ship do not offer the same effect. In many ways, out of sight equals out of mind. As such, if a country chooses to pull its airplanes or ships, the impact is not the same. They do not hold ground so allies are not required to fill in a large hole. Moreover, as the risk is lower, it is easier to find other donor nations willing to fill in the gap. In the end, boots on the ground, even when explained as a "quick in and out" can translate into a prolonged, very expensive, and very costly, commitment to a seemingly endless conflict. One need only look to the Balkan and Afghanistan examples.

32   The effect and consequences of military engagement are pronounced. For example, former Chief of the Defence Staff (CDS) General Hillier explained that when the International Security Assistance Force (ISAF) was originally established, Canada was not invited to join. He explained, "The Europeans wouldn't let us join ISAF. Canada desperately wanted to join ISAF at the start of the war in Afghanistan, but we were shunned. Part of the reason was that the Europeans, the British in particular, remembered our risk-averse approach in Bosnia and had no faith that Canada would pull its weight, especially if things got tough. They did not want us as part of their alliance." He elaborated, "As far as they were concerned, Canada could not be relied upon to do the tough stuff and was therefore of no use. The British Command structure remembered

the years in the former Yugoslavia when 'Can't bat' – Canada's contribution to the UN, and later to NATO, forces – needed days or even weeks
to get approval from Ottawa before we would take on an operation, assuming we were even allowed to do so. The Canadian government, which
desperately wanted to join the ISAF operation, was paying the price for
its risk-averse, micromanaging approach to military overseas operations."
General Rick Hillier, *A Soldier First. Bullets, Bureaucrats and the Politics
of War* (Toronto: HarperCollins Publishers Ltd., 2009), 159 and 473. Iraq
in 2003, as already discussed, was another example of negative consequences for failing to engage. What makes this frustrating is the fact that
although Canada contributed to the larger American "war on terrorism"
and committed ships and planes to the effort, including the Arabian
Gulf, because it refused to commit ground troops to the invasion of Iraq,
it was largely shunned by the Americans and they did not acknowledge
the Canadian contribution. Conversely, Canada's support to Afghanistan
was highly beneficial to the country. An American request to redeploy
a special operations task force (SOTF) in 2005, was strongly supported
by both the then CDS, General Hillier, and the deputy minister, D. M.
Elcock. They explained, "The deployment of Canadian special operations
forces to Afghanistan would make evident our ongoing commitment to
an active engagement in the Campaign Against Terrorism and it would
also demonstrate our direct burden sharing with our closest allies." More
recently, on 14 February 2012, the MND announced a meeting with his
German counterpart Thomas de Maiziere and that Canada secured a deal
with Germany to establish a strategic European base that would support future conflict. It followed a very low-key media announcement the
previous day that a German company had signed a deal with Canada
to provide one of the potential designs for the navy's new joint supply
ships.

33   This is the official Canadian Special Operations Forces Command
doctrinal definition. Special operations differ from conventional operations in the degree of physical and political risk, operational techniques,
modes of employment, independence from friendly support and dependence on detailed operational intelligence. Canada, *CANSOFCOM
Capstone Concept for Special Operations 2009* (Ottawa: DND, 2009), 4.

34   CANSOFCOM *Capstone Concept for Special Operations* 2009, 4.

35   Department of National Defence, *Canadian Special Operations Forces Command: An Overview* (DND: Ottawa, 2008), 9.

36   "Non-Kinetic" options refer to a wide range of skills and task sets that include provision of strategic advisory teams, security force assistance, information operations, psychological operations, and support to other military, paramilitary or law enforcement agencies.

37   "Chapter 11 – Special Operations," *NATO Publication AJP-1 (A)*, Third Draft, March 1998, 11-1.

CHAPTER 2

WHOLE OF GOVERNMENT OPERATIONS IN THE CONTEMPORARY SECURITY ENVIRONMENT

DR. HOWARD G. COOMBS

The primary challenge in unconventional conflicts is political-psychological, multi-dimensional, and rarely susceptible to single-component strategies or orthodox political-military operations. While all wars are political and psychological, in unconventional conflicts military operations quickly and pervasively take on political and psychological dimensions, often placing military operations in second place.[1]

Sam Sarkesian
Unconventional Conflicts in a New Security Era

The late Professor Sam Sarkesian, a renowned soldier-scholar, noted that his experience as a United States Army officer in Korea and Vietnam, as well as extensive study into unconventional and revolutionary warfare, had led him to believe that complicated low intensity conflicts were only susceptible to multifaceted efforts that included political and psychological activities to neutralize or deter disintegrating forces.[2] When examining western efforts in Afghanistan one is struck by the accuracy of this statement. NATO's adoption of the "comprehensive approach" to provide unity of effort amongst a myriad of organizations and nations is mirrored by the United States "interagency" paradigm and the United Kingdom's "joined-up approach". Canadian efforts over the last few years to implement a "whole of government" construct, in addition to the Canadian Army's efforts to put into action a supporting doctrine of "Joint, International, Multi-Agency and Public" (JIMP) activity are all part of this movement.

Canada's whole of government effort had its roots in the defence, diplomacy, development plus commerce (3D+C) model of the early 21st century. The idea of the interrelationship between defence, diplomacy, development plus commerce matured in the crucible of governmental involvement in the International Security Assistance Force mission in Afghanistan. The idea of networks of friendly entities creating a shared vision and common intent in order to neutralize and overcome opposing influences, in addition to ensuring that the support of neutrals remained unaligned or was swayed to throw in with the Afghan government and its allies was captured in counter-insurgency (COIN) doctrine as "population-centric COIN".

Subsequently, conceptual approaches arose that catered to the exigencies of population-centric COIN. Understanding the environment – human and physical – neutralizing opposing forces, securing communities and their surrounding areas, and increasing capacity are the foundation of these efforts. Much work has been put into understanding the relationship between various COIN forces, including the burgeoning role of special operations forces along with other enabling forces,[3] and their employment in this complex form of "war amongst the people."[4]

CANADIAN COIN EFFORTS IN AFGHANISTAN[5]

From September 2010 to July 2011 the last rotation of Task Force Kandahar led Canada's combat mission in southern Afghanistan. Using hard won knowledge gained from successive Canadian deployments in this region, fundamentals of the COIN campaign were explicitly laid out. Building on the experiences of previous rotations it was understood that a number of underlying principles needed to be internalized within all our forces pursuing population-centric operations.

Firstly, the requirement to prosecute this conflict with vigour and perseverance was difficult in a setting where the opposing forces were not easy to discern, define and defeat. It was not possible to orient operations into bringing opposing forces to a decisive physical and or moral engagement resulting in an unambiguous victory. This was, and is, a protracted conflict requiring a delicate touch that balanced military activities with the needs of the people for governance, reconstruction and development.

Secondly, following from those demands, was the requirement to coordinate and concentrate power – physical, psychological and cybernetic. While this principle was well understood, it was extremely complicated to execute in an environment that embraced a huge number of influences. These pressures included the activities of numerous military and non-military actors who were attempting to stabilize Afghanistan and build national capacity in a host of areas. On top of that was the impact of a population divided and fractured by over three decades of constant violence, lacking confidence in themselves and central governance. Furthermore, there existed a whole host of disintegrating influences both domestic and international. At the local level this ranged across multiple challenges, from malign actors of all types, through illicit activities to insurgents, which in turn combined to fuel the lack of assurance exhibited by the rest of the world in the ability of Afghans to administer their own affairs. This latter lack of international confidence continues today and grows to fuel the other disintegrating influences.

Thirdly, the appetite of both Afghans and contributing NATO nations for the seemingly never-ending and inconclusive struggle currently taking place in southwest Asia has resulted in a public desire to diminish military contributions and achieve a positive conclusion rapidly – most recently by very publicly touted international exit strategies aligned with an end date of 2014. This espoused end-date has focused the efforts of both the international community and the Government of the Islamic Republic of Afghanistan (GIRoA) to accomplish as much as possible in the short time remaining in various western mandates.

Fourthly, any military victories gained must be immediately followed up with persistent security, both military and police, in the form of the Afghan National Security Forces (ANSF), some type of functioning governance, as well as reconstruction and development efforts designed to support national and sub-national economies. Canada's most recent contributions to the war in Afghanistan are training these forces as part of the NATO Training Mission Afghanistan (NTM-A), but Task Force Kandahar also expended a great deal of time in conjunction with combat operations training and mentoring their affiliated Afghanistan National Army (ANA) formation, the 1st Brigade, 205 Corps (1/205), in addition to similar efforts with the local Afghanistan National Police (ANP).

Consequently, threats to military and other forces, as well as dangers to the population were confronted directly and indirectly in a manner that destroyed, neutralized or disrupted them. The activities carried out by Canadian and other coalition forces included combat operations, normally in partnership with the ANA and ANP, countering improvised explosive devices, establishing enhanced security in populated regions, and implementing procedures designed to restrict the movement of insurgents throughout the Canadian area of responsibility. These control measures included checkpoints on major routes in conjunction with barriers designed to limit the transport of people and materials away from these primary roads with their restricted access points and enhanced security.

As a result of the requirements of this complex contemporary environment, Canadian military activities in southern Afghanistan were conducted in a manner that reflected the recent evolution of counter-insurgency theory and practice. Western forces have moved from operational designs aimed at countering Maoist interpretations of armed struggle to supporting present whole of government efforts aimed at creating regionally tailored solutions along multiple and focused lines of effort. These actions are also in keeping with the precepts of what I like to think of as DEFINE-SHAPE-SECURE-HOLD-BUILD (and ENABLE) partially articulated in recent American and Canadian doctrine as CLEAR-HOLD-BUILD, but more so practiced in a form like this more detailed model. In accordance with these ideas, COIN practitioners, like David Kilcullen, have suggested that (1) it is necessary to develop a fulsome understanding of the reasons behind the conflict in a specific area or population, and (2) in conjunction with this knowledge one must put the welfare of the local people ahead of any other consideration – even killing the enemy. In this fashion, by partnering with the people and developing genuine and respectful relationships, one convinces populations that the counter-insurgent will be victorious and, thus, is able to separate the insurgent from their population base.[6] In that vein, Task Force Kandahar's efforts to fight the insurgent were successful, but in that process it was well understood that while fighting the insurgent is relatively easy, defeating the insurgency is much more challenging. The successes of Canadian military operations, in combination with the surge of American forces across Kandahar (and elsewhere), created the space necessary to permit the GIRoA and its allies to address the roots of the insurgency in southern Afghanistan. The proof of this approach was visible in that the level and efficacy of insurgent violence within the Canadian area of responsibility had been much reduced from previous years during the months preceding the July 2011 transfer of authority between Canadian and American forces.

To accomplish these effects Task Force Kandahar expended a great deal of effort in information gathering and analysis. This focus was necessary in order to understand the constantly evolving political, military, economic, social, informational and infrastructural dimensions of the local environment. In turn, that knowledge permitted the types of capacity building efforts aimed at strengthening and stabilizing the local districts. By partnering and mentoring the ANSF, Afghan army and police, Task Force Kanda-har assisted with the ongoing processes of professionalization and increasing Afghan facility with security operations. The ANA is a rapidly expanding institution, seen by many local Afghans as representative of their nation, and viewed by some insurgents as an effective opposition.[7] At the same time, the ANP has further to go before they are considered successful, however, they are slowly improving. This progress will continue as numbers grow and more police receive training in the fundamentals of being a peace officer and learning to support their jurisdictions through the rule of law. Our current efforts with NTM-A recognize this requirement.

In addition to the hard work being put into the ANSF, Task Force Kandahar worked closely with our field partners, amongst whom the Department of Foreign Affairs and International Trade and the Canadian International Development Agency (CIDA) are prominent in encouraging governance and development. The Representative of Canada in Kandahar (RoCK), Tim Martin, was not only the se-nior Canadian civilian government official in the province, he was also the Director of the Kandahar Provincial Reconstruction Team (KPRT) for the majority of the last combat rotation. His group of American and Canadian representatives worked to assist Afghan provincial and district officials with issues related to the estab-lishment of comprehensive governance and development from the village to provincial levels. They also assisted through the Head of Mission – the Canadian Ambassador William Crosbie – in link-ing these provincial concerns to the central government in Kabul. Task Force Kandahar contributed to these whole of government efforts by facilitating these issues within villages and districts inclusive to its assigned area of Kandahar – Panjwa'i, Dand and Daman – and by linking immediate tactical gains to the sustain-able programs and policies of GIRoA through the KPRT. The net effect was that one was able to make a large difference in extending stability by unifying the actions of all involved agencies within an overarching security context. This approach addressed the disin-tegrating influences affecting the Canadian portion of southern

Afghanistan in a regional and coordinated manner that enabled the prioritization and allocation of resources. Furthermore, this approach brought sufficient resources to bear in the villages and village clusters, demonstrating to the Afghan people the commitment of the GIRoA and the international community vis-à-vis national reconstruction and state building.

This method of negating the insurgency was local in nature and attempted to create functioning districts through an integrated effort targeting specific villages and groupings of villages for substantial governmental and developmental intervention. These locations were and are connected to national and provincial programs, urban, market, transportation and trade development packages, and local security sector reform activity. This prioritization also permitted security forces to allocate their resources in the best manner to create a secure environment for those involved with these governmental, reconstruction and development activities.

Consequently, Task Force Kandahar and its interagency collaborators fought the insurgency in a number of ways. Canadian military efforts in Southern Afghanistan were oriented towards removing destabilizing influences, and establishing and maintaining population (community)-centric security. This created the conditions for an integrated interagency approach that generated and promoted local governance and development, mostly from the bottom-up. As part of this the whole-of-government effort, wherever possible one reinforces and, where necessary establishes, partnerships that put Afghan officials and security forces in the forefront and the population's interests first. Once appropriate conditions were established, like responsible and functioning governance, burgeoning local economies with a rural/urban interface and a capable ANSF, those districts would be ready to transition to complete Afghan control – and indeed, Dand, one of the former Canadian districts, is high on the list for transition of control from NATO-supported to wholly Afghan-led.

CHAPTER 2

In order to deal with the complexity of population-centric COIN, the Canadian Forces in Afghanistan (1) fought the insurgent and, more importantly, (2) attempted to address the dissatisfaction that led to the insurgency. While the former was, and is, mostly a se-curity problem, the latter is much more challenging and requires a concerted effort in the areas of governance and development, otherwise any military success will be illusory. Interestingly, Spe-cial Operations Forces, amongst the actors already delineated, also played an important role in both these efforts.

SPECIAL OPERATIONS FORCES IN COIN

Canadian Special Operations Forces Command operations abroad strive to:

a. destroy, disorganize, and disrupt the networks of violent organizations;

b. degrade and deny access of violent organizations to the nation's population;

c. construct social networks to promote legitimacy of efforts; and

d. organize, enable, and improve partner's tactical and operational skills in counter-terrorism (CT).[8]

This excerpt from a 2010 Canadian Department of National Defence doctrinal publication captures the gamut of activities conducted by special operations forces in support of counter-insurgency. Spe-cial operations teams, like conventional forces, aimed at attacking the insurgent and the insurgency. Special operations forces were a significant contributor to the activities of Task Force Kandahar in three main areas: Firstly, aggressive targeting of insurgent com-mand and control across ISAF assisted greatly with decapitating the insurgency; secondly, special operations forces complemented conventional operations through (1) targeting Afghan compounds of interest and (2) Village Stability Operations (VSO) and supporting operations; and lastly, of great significance were special operations forces' efforts at capacity building in the realm of ANP training and mentoring.

The directed targeting of insurgent leaders and their principal networks have become an important mission for special operations forces in Afghanistan. While population-centric COIN focuses on increasing security presence and the building of host-nation institutions, it is still necessary to decapitate the insurgent effort by removing the people and means that allow for decisions to be made and orders to be passed to insurgent cells. These missions degraded the insurgent command structure to such an extent that it was left with little ability to effect coherent and coordinated operations. In addition to this, special operations forces assist conventional forces with special reconnaissance, like continuous observation and reporting of potential insurgent locations, in order to delineate potential objectives and permit timely security force action to take place. On top of this, security initiatives in the local communities increased Task Force Kandahar effectiveness. VSO initiatives, such as the Afghanistan Local Police (ALP), provided increasing security within villages and village clusters, by creating community-based defence forces that would protect the population from outside incursion and were linked to the government through the local ANP. Finally, special operations forces support to capacity building assisted the ANP in creating a response capability capable of reacting effectively to *in extremis* situations.

However, despite all the positive aspects of special operations forces, several cautions must be drawn. Control of these forces is retained centrally at the highest levels, in a similar fashion to aerospace power, and permits the implementation of decentralized tactical activities that have strategic impact. In certain ways this model grew out of the linear, synchronous joint battlespace of the

Cold War, when it was anticipated that within the Joint Operating Area multiple forces could be parsed out and controlled centrally by a Joint Task Force Commander. Special operations, like the other components such as Maritime, Land and Air, would be assigned portions of the Joint Operating Area, with coordination being effected by the Joint Task Force Headquarters. This model worked extremely well during Operations DESERT SHIELD and DESERT STORM, as well as in the opening phases of Operations ENDURING FREEDOM and IRAQI FREEDOM. However, as the joint battlespace became cluttered in both Afghanistan and Iraq, it was more non-linear and asynchronous than not, and multiple friendly entities operated in the same area, mostly harmoniously, but at times with an apparent lack of information sharing or coordination that created disastrous results. As in the recent 2012 uninformed burning of Korans at Bagram Airfield, outside Kabul, such missteps can have far reaching consequences.[9] Almost a year earlier, during a 2011 United States special operations forces-led night raid, Afghan President Hamid Karzai's cousin was mistakenly killed, in the village of Karz, Dand district, within the Canadian area of responsibility.[10] While the events surrounding the raid remain classified, it was not ever made clear whether the forces that were inserted into the area were fully aware of the human terrain. If that was a contributing factor to this event it was an oversight that could easily have been rectified by prior interaction and coordination with the in-place conventional forces and the NATO-supported Afghan leadership and security forces.

Whatever the cause, the impact of this misstep was enormous. The ISAF Commander General David Petraeus, in the face of Afghan public outcry, had publicly apologized a week or so prior to this event for the deaths of a number of children mistakenly killed by NATO in Eastern Afghanistan. This apology was meant to not only publicly atone for a horrific mistake but also to assuage President Karzai, whose very evident concern about civilian casualties and special operations' night raids had been widely reported. In one instant this apology was rendered meaningless. As well, the aftermath of this event diminished Karzai in the eyes of many Afghans. He was a perceived as a leader who had no ability to secure the safety of his own family let alone protect the lives of his countrymen from NATO depredations. Furthermore, as local repercussion of the incident, the District Leader of Dand, Ahmidullah Nazek, publicly noted that it was difficult to maintain credibility with his people if it was believed that he had no influence on or awareness of the activities of NATO security forces within his district. In short, the event was a public coup for the insurgent forces.

Accordingly, the need to ensure coordination at the lowest levels of conventional and unconventional forces needs to be re-examined in the command and control arrangements for special operations forces. While the requirement of special operations forces to be controlled at the highest level remains, the concomitant need that low level coordination be compelled to take place with in-place forces as part of special operations forces command and control architecture also exists, particularly when a misstep, or tragic error, has widespread consequences at local and national levels, in addition to negative strategic implications. It is evident to me that the current approach, originally imbued in doctrine as a result a battlespace framework devised during the Cold War for large scale conventional conflict, does not always work well in the contemporary environment.

Another perceived challenge for special operations forces in the multifaceted operations of today's security environment lies within the very nature of special operations. Former American special operator, Professor Hy Rothestein argues that special operations have two dimensions: direct action and unconventional warfare. The former are those missions of limited duration against high value targets normally for operational (theatre) or strategic effects. The latter role encompasses any effort where special operations forces work with the indigenous forces and local population.[11] From my perspective the types of organizations and, more

importantly, people that do these various missions are not necessarily the same. While population-centric COIN demands CT
activities, as well as the interdiction and destruction of opposing
networks in order to render insurgents leaderless, the need for capacity building amongst the local people and their security forces
is also incredibly important. Exacerbating this situation are the
limited numbers of special operators available to fulfil both sets of
tasks. Thus, we have seen over the last ten years the rapid expan-
sion of numbers of those considered special operations forces to
fulfil both sets of activities. This need for special operators has
not only resulted in a speedy and, what some would consider,
unbridled growth but at times interchanging forces that have
been primarily associated with direct action missions to more unconventional warfare capacity building roles, with, as one would
expect, variable results. The culture of direct action is not that of
unconventional warfare and senior military commanders must be
sensitized to that employment challenge. Also, the rapid enlarge-
ment in the special operations forces community of the pool of
units that have been drawn on to contribute to the special forces
unconventional warfare capacity must be reconsidered – working
with a host nation, like Afghanistan, requires high levels of cultural and emotional skills, in addition to being proficient in one's
métier, and not all organizations have those capacities. Without
considering these intangible factors in the designation of those
who are included in the context of special operations forces, one
incurs great risk in assigning inappropriate forces to one of the
most important population-centric COIN activities, that of host-
nation capacity building.

On a related note, and one that gets little discussion, is the no-
tion, just mentioned, that the culture of direct action missions is
not that of unconventional warfare. The reliance on special operations forces to conduct direct action has, from my perspective,
created amongst segments of the special operations communities,
an outlook sometimes inimical to the other unconventional and
conventional activities and, at times, increased tensions with

various COIN forces supposedly fighting to create the same outcomes. While only a personal belief, I suggest that this is an issue that bears further scrutiny as NATO activities in Afghanistan draw to a close.

CONCLUSION

...we will create mission success and strategic effect as an integrated force and through core service and formation competencies when our naval, land, air, and special operations forces support each other in operations. With our Defence team we will forge relationships and work with allies, other government departments, and international and non-governmental organizations.[12]

Indeed this will be Canada's true legacy in Afghanistan: that the service and sacrifices of military and civilian personnel have assisted with creating conditions for a stable and secure nation. The impact of these efforts in assisting the Afghan people will far outlast our presence and contribute to an ultimate goal of securing Afghanistan's future as a functioning member of the international community. Underpinning this is the great deal of hard-won knowledge and experience that has been gained, starting with the need to recognize that in population-centric counter-insurgency one cannot kill their way to victory.

The Canadian Forces have learned and relearned a great deal through their activities in Afghanistan. The implementation of a comprehensive Canadian intergovernmental approach to addressing the complex dilemmas of the contemporary environment has been vital to any achievements that we have experienced. These processes have included the Department of Foreign Affairs and International Trade and the Canadian International Development Agency, as well as other governmental organizations like the Royal Canadian Mounted Police and Corrections Services Canada. Conducting a military counter-insurgency in the context of

Afghanistan is just one piece of the overall puzzle and makes no sense without the other parts. In what I like to call the paradoxical trinity of whole of government operations (1) development cannot take place without the existence of a secure environment, (2) security without governance lacks purpose, and (3) governance without development and reconstruction will not persist.

From this it becomes quickly evident that population-centric COIN requires integration of all activities, both military and non-military, to combat the insurgent and the insurgency. Establishing a common vision and intent is a large part of this integration and in order to do this requires a great deal of hard work and perseverance.

In this battle of wills, special operations forces are amongst a group of select enabling elements that can act to facilitate integration amongst this myriad of actors. They do this through assisting with capacity building within the host nation and helping to connect peoples and groups of like minds to central government and in this fashion combat the insurgency. At the same time, special operations forces fight the insurgent through direct action missions and by supporting security force operations through reconnaissance and other missions. In the course of these activities it has been recognized by all participants that special operations forces are a powerful force multiplier in the contemporary security environment. At the same time it must also be noted that careful consideration must be given to special operations forces command and control arrangements in order to carefully select those forces to be deemed special operations capable and to make certain that special operations forces elements are accurately matched to the various tasks that they are assigned. Only in this fashion can one ensure that optimal results are achieved from special operations forces in the complicated and complex environments of 21st century war amongst the people.

NOTES

1   Sam Sarkesian, *Unconventional Conflicts in a New Security Era: Lessons from Malaya and Vietnam* (Westport, CT: Greenwood, 1993), 22. With thanks to Colonel (Ret.) David Maxwell, US Army, Associate Director Center for Peace and Security Studies & Security Studies Program, Edmund A. Walsh School of Foreign Service, Georgetown University for providing this reference.

2   John Allen Williams, "The Inter-University Seminar on Armed Forces and Society: Sam C. Sarkesian – 1927-2011" [web page] <http://memorial.iusafs.net/sarkesian.html>; accessed 19 February 2012.

3   Other critical enablers are Civil-Military Cooperation (CIMIC), Information Operations and Psychological Operations (PSYOPs). These teams are in Canadian doctrine contained under the conceptual approach "Influence Activities." The United States uses the title "Military Information Support Operations" (MISO) to contain the latter two activities, while CIMIC is still separated. Interestingly in the US MISO is for the most part intertwined with Special Operations Forces.

4   This phrase gained recent popularity as a result of General Sir Rupert Smith's book, *The Utility of Force: The Art of War in the Modern World* (London: Penguin Books Ltd., 2005). In this work Smith questions the efficacy of violence, or the "utility of force" in modern peoples' wars. On page 331 he opines that "For unlike industrial war, in war amongst the people no act of force will ever be decisive: winning the trial of strength will not deliver the will of the people, and at base that is the only true aim of any use of force in our modern conflicts." These thoughts along other modern practitioners, like Sir Robert Thompson (Malaya) and Lieutenant-Colonel David Galula (Algeria), inform current counter-insurgency theory and practices.

5   This section is adapted from Dr. Howard Coombs and Brigadier-General Dean Milner, "Canada's Counter Insurgency in Afghanistan," *On Track* 15, No. 4 (Winter 2010/2011): 23-25.

6   David Kilcullen, *Counterinsurgency* (New York: Oxford University Press, 2010), 3-4.

7   "Lunch with the Taliban: Recent hopes of a negotiated peace are overblown," *The Economist* [journal on-line], available at <http://www.economist.com/node/17363902>; accessed 18 November 2010, n.p.

8   Canada, Department of National Defence, *B-GJ-005-300/FP-001 Canadian Forces Joint Publication (CFJP) 3.0 Operations* (2010), para 0331, p. 3-7.

9   Alissa J. Rubin, "Chain of Avoidable Errors Cited in Koran Burning" *The New York Times* (March 2, 2012) [newspaper on-line], available at <http://www.nytimes.com/2012/03/03/world/asia/5-soldiers-are-said-to-face-punishment-in-koran-burning-in-afghanistan.html?pagewanted=all>; accessed 11 March 2012.

10   One article from the period is Keith Gerein, "NATO investigates killing of Karzai's cousin," *The Vancouver Sun* (March 10, 2011) [newspaper on-line], available at <http://www.vancouversun.com/news/partner/shell/NATO+investigates+killing+Karzai+cousin/4415359/story.html>; accessed 11 March 2012. An internet search of the topic will access many sources discussing this event.

11   Hy S. Rothstein, *Afghanistan and the Troubled Future of Unconventional Warfare*, foreword by Seymour Hersh (Annapolis, Maryland: Naval Institute Press, 2006), 175.

12   Canada, Department of National Defence, "Foreword", *B-GJ-005-300/FP-001 Canadian Forces Joint Publication (CFJP) 3.0 Operations* (2010), v.

CHAPTER 3

STRATEGIC MESSAGING

COLONEL MIKE ROULEAU

Let me begin by exposing my weaknesses and bias upfront on the important issue of strategic messaging. First, in terms of DDMA depth, I am limited by having grown up in Joint Task Force 2 (JTF 2). Moreover, my command positions within that unit always forced me to view the exercise of outward strategic communication from a decidedly defensive perspective. Success rested in what did *not* attract media interest rather than projecting a positive self-image within the media. Nonetheless, although throughout my military career I have not acted as a DDMA or strategic communication authority, I have spent the past three years engaged in academic endeavours that pertain to organizational growth and strategic messaging. As such, as an experienced operator and commander and a nascent academic, I provide a valuable and unique perspective on the issue at hand that is above all a special operations forces practitioner's point of view.

My conclusion is simply espoused but arguably more difficult to administer: strategic communication is vital to the long run sustainability of Canadian Special Operations Forces Command because it enhances its legitimacy externally while making it a smarter, more coherent organization internally. In order to appreciate the validity of this statement, one must first understand why strategic communication matters to SOF, why it is hard to do well and, finally, what all this means for CANSOFCOM as it continues to grow and develop.

The main reason that strategic communication is essential to SOF is that it helps to foster both internal and external legitimacy. To explain this point, I will rely on ideas brought forth in sociologist Richard Scott's Institutional Analysis work. Without getting into detail around how organizations grow and develop, a few salient facts must nonetheless be addressed. The first is that military organizations essentially arise from regulatory decisions. For example, for a military organization to be stood-up, the establishment of an entity through a Ministerial Organization Order and subsequently a Canadian Forces Organization Order establishing it in the CF's Order of Battle is required. From that point forward, the race is on. Second, once established, organizations embark on the never-ending quest to attain institutional status – the process of grounding transactional organizational activities within a much deeper foundation where the internal social fabric comes to life. Because new organizations like CANSOFCOM are born into an already established CF and national security ecosystem, they naturally assume part of an extant "market share" within this community. In this maturation phase, other institutions may be displaced. As such, credibility and social acceptability are vitally important for organizations as they compete for "market shares". Finally, this quest for legitimacy requires, as one of its main enablers, a robust strategic communication approach with both in-reach and outreach elements to it. The bottom line to this point is that strategic communication should be thought of as the canvas to paint one's story on and, at the strategic level in Defence Headquarters, the ability to succinctly "tell a story" is an invaluable art that helps to move things forward.

Naturally, developing a strategic communication plan stimulates internal dialogue. Its very formulation forces key leaders to the table for a series of all-important brainstorming sessions with the purpose of coalescing ideas around the Commander's vision and perhaps even refining or maturing the vision.

Moreover, the act of setting about thinking of strategic communication is the first step toward establishing a culture that recognizes that – and potentially how – the institution affects the external environment and conversely that the external environment buffets the institution. As such, it becomes recognized that "out there" and "in here" are indeed parts of a single ecosystem.

In order to operationalize things, it is important at this point to unpack the word "strategy". Strategy is nothing more than a prudent set of ideas for employing one's instruments in an integrated and synchronized fashion to achieve objectives. Strategy links what needs to be accomplished (ends), with how to accomplish it (ways), with the resources needed to accomplish them (means). In this way, strategy highlights risks, mutually links activities and prioritizes finite resources in the context of a rigorous appreciation of the environment.

Clearly, strategic communication is not the answer to establishing CANSOFCOM's strategy – that is a separate piece – but strategic communication is a cross-cutting activity that drives horizontally through whatever pillars a strategy possess. In soldier speak: it is a supporting plan.

Despite the obvious importance of having a good strategic communication plan, it is not easy to do, particularly for SOF. CANSOFCOM is an emerging organization full of superb "doers" at the tactical level. Over its six years of existence, and indeed in the fourteen preceding years with JTF 2, its tactical and operational actions at home and around the world have garnered strategic effect for the CF, Department of National Defence and the Government of Canada. But the relevant question remains: have these tactical and operational successes been planned, executed and cycled back into the institution, incorporating strategic communication as a deliberate element of our thinking? I suspect the answer is not entirely.

One of the major challenges to this goal is operations security (OPSEC). OPSEC is lifeblood to successful special operations outcomes. A cursory historical examination back to the Second World War that looks at the Special Operations Executive, the Office of Strategic Services or more recently, at the Balkans, Iraq, Afghanistan and elsewhere demonstrate this connection to be true. Indeed, those of us who entered the community before 11 September 2001 (9/11) were indoctrinated in a very singular OPSEC culture: you needed it, all the time, full stop.

As CANSOFCOM has grown from JTF 2's humble beginnings, it follows that its strategic communication culture, or lack thereof, takes as its frame of reference that very singular perspective: everything pertains to OPSEC. Unfortunately, this vision may be rooted in a negative point of view – "what do we want to avoid" while the future strategic and security environment calls for a positive communication vision – "what do we want to gain."

A second challenges is that the tyranny of the urgent always trumps grander, more strategic issues like strategic communication. While the Canadian Forces made huge progress in a post-Somalia and Balkans era of the later 1990s, the events of 9/11 consumed our focus at the tactical level of war. In this context, JTF 2, then CANSOFCOM, engaged their energies decisively at ensuring her forces were enabled for sustained success in the battlespace, largely in the Direct Action and Special Reconnaissance roles up until 2009. Thinking substantively in the strategic communication realm was not at the top of anyone's list in CANSOFCOM. As a case in point, I offer a quick anecdote from my time as a Special Operations Task Force Commander in early 2007: the mission was to capture or kill a Medium Value Target to the northeast of Kandahar City. The targeting and mission approvals were duly conducted with my in theatre chain of command and the mission was appropriately de-conflicted with the "battlespace owner", Commander Regional Command South (Comd RC(S)), Dutch Major-General Van Loon. The mission was successful, bringing the target into custody for further exploitation. Minutes after the force recovered to the FOB, I received a call from none other than Comd RC(S) himself who was extremely pleased with the outcome because it would yield a decidedly positive effect for the region as a whole. He told me he wanted to proceed with an international press release to leverage the success. To be honest, I had not even contemplated such a possibility. The strategic communication upside to what we were doing was something I rarely spent much time considering as a function of it not being my job – someone else would take care of that. I had more tactical challenges to face ... In five seconds, I blurted out that he should fill his boots – just don't mention CANSOF please.

This example leads to my third and final observation on why we potentially underperform in the realm of strategic communication – we *do* a lot and because of that we *think* less. And we think *critically* even less. Time is certainly a limiting factor. I do not mean to imply that CANSOF is devoid of thoughtfulness because it is clearly not. But there are human and cognitive limits to the breadth of issues that can be substantively advanced in a certain period of time under stressful circumstances and I submit that because the average CF commander is raised to preference all things operational, we have bypassed strategic communication. Moreover, perhaps we remain unconditioned to include communications specialists like Public Affairs Officers as early in the operational planning process as we should.

Regardless of cause, neither the strategic context of an information-rich Western democracy like Canada nor the future security environment will be particularly hospitable to organizations who do not fully embrace a thoughtful strategic communication culture. The advent of "fourth generation warfare" or "compound or hybrid warfare" as some call it is changing the landscape. Confronting illusive threats in the context of a simultaneous nation building enterprise have forced SOF and conventional commanders to revisit the OPSEC paradigm. Contemporary officers and troopers are every bit as talented as our forefathers in waging war and they are continuously adapting mission planning, synchronization and execution to cater to supporting indigenous forces or contending with time-sensitive targets and so on. Realities on the ground force tactical creativity – that is just what military forces do to stay among the living. But strategic communication, in the sense I am treating it, does not *start* at the tactical level. It cycles through the tactical level starting from and returning to the institutional level where directional handrails are provided and context is given. In other words, you cannot develop strategic communication at the coalface but it is only once that tactical level buys in that you can achieve a strategic communication cultural shift. And this, as all cultural shifts do, should be expected to take time to develop.

Having looked at some of the reasons why embracing a strategic communication culture is inherently challenging for SOF, let me close with a few thought that may be useful moving ahead. First, CANSOFCOM needs to internalize the opportunity costs of potentially underperforming in the area of strategic communication writ large. The leap from organizational status to becoming an institution requires a thickening of the CANSOFCOM brand which in turn adds reputational gravitas acting as a hedge against inevitable future challenges. This "thickening" cannot develop so long as Canada's SOF remain too veiled so the issue then becomes one of calculated choice on what is considered OPSEC and what is releasable information.

Second, the Command should always shape strategic thought around the organizing principle of "aspiration" vice "fear". The former is a positivist arc that unleashes creative energy and is, by definition, oriented to the long-term. The latter is decidedly defensive, protectionist and *ad hoc* treating only issues-of-the-day. Frankly, there is too much upside in CANSOFCOM to not be bullish about getting some of the good word out in a more deliberate way.

Third, CANSOFCOM should continue to foster a culture of strategic thinking that has at its core an entrepreneurial bent to constantly exploit opportunities by leading with speed. In that sense it needs to continue embracing risk-taking while remaining highly sensitive to its internal and external environments.

The fourth point is a precondition for the preceding strategic thinking culture point. The Command should seek continued improvement in the domain of critical thinking. Authors like Peter Senge and his work *The Fifth Discipline* teach us the inherent value of parking – truly parking – biases around the leader-ship table which is the only way to transition from participative openness – where people talk to each other – toward reflective openness – listening to each other in a way that inspires shared commitment. What Senge says forces us to be introspective about how our experiences and perspectives limit our thinking and sometimes contribute to exacerbating challenge areas.[1]

The fifth point is a natural extension to critical thinking and that is how we visually explain our story. Edward Tufte, a noted aca-demic in this field, has some terrific thoughts on the issue that add layers of richness and texture to portraying one's case. This depth is vitally important at the military strategic level where time and attention pressures abound and so clarity and context are the order of the day. Sometimes leaders will "believe it when they see it" and other times "they'll believe it when they see it". The difference is not so subtle but both conditions demand a clear picture.

In closing, I offer a final comment. CANSOFCOM has a level of individual talent among its ranks that is the envy of most. This talent is the benefit of having rigorous screening and selection processes but the trick moving ahead is to channel it into kinetic energy around some concentrated philosophies and strategies. In that sense, a strategic communication culture would not only enhance operational outputs, it would do much to adding to

CANSOFCOM's legitimacy – something at the heart of long-term sustainability. I see this as a natural and necessary progression and further institutionalization of a vibrant CANSOFCOM within a strong CF.

NOTES

1   Peter M. Serge, *The Fifth Discipline: The Art & Practice of the Learning Organization* (US: Doubleday, 2006).

CHAPTER 4

SOME CHALLENGES
OF TRAINING OTHERS

US BRIGADIER-GENERAL (RETIRED) HECTOR PAGAN

The United States and her allies have long recognized the value of building global partnerships. Nonetheless, the reality of the contemporary operational environment, including deployments to Iraq and Afghanistan, has affected the US's ability to maintain its pre-11 September 2001 level of presence in many countries. The value of training others remains undiminished, however. This paper deals with some of the challenges associated with this endeavour.

To understand the challenges of training others it is first important to examine why and how we perform this activity. From an American perspective, we help shape the security environment by training others for two main reasons: first, to help build partner nation capacity and, second to develop and maintain close contacts with our friends in the region. It is believed that each contributes to a more stable geo-political environment.

American special operations forces help shape the security environment by working in concert with our interagency partners and coordinating closely with the country team. At this point it is essential to stress that not only do we coordinate all missions with the US embassy, but we also do our best to support the ambassador's country strategy. Additionally, more often than not, the theatre special operations command maintains some level of presence to coordinate those activities and provide command and control forward. As such, this lengthy process involves coordination with the embassy, the partner nation, the host unit, and the combatant command. Moreover, several other steps take place at the Joint Staff level to help coordinate these deployments and maintain visibility and accountability of all forces.

Notably, activities across the combatant command's area of operations do not happen in a vacuum. Deployments have a specific purpose and support the Combatant Commander's objectives. The four star combatant commander will publish his/her theatre engagement strategy or campaign plan and every component commander, including the theatre special operations command, will publish a supporting plan to this strategy, taking into consideration the commander's objectives, available resources, funds and, most importantly, people.

The US Special Operations Command (USSOCOM) does its parallel planning to support these activities worldwide. The Theatre Special Operations Command matches requirements with assets and tries to cover as much ground as possible. In Latin America, for example, the main task is building partner nation capacity to counter trans-national crime, especially illicit trafficking activities. Certainly, a lot happens before you put boots on the ground.

Throughout this process, it is important to maintain focus and remember that we train others to achieve a cumulative effect brought about by training activities that should build upon previous missions and work within a regional, and ultimately global, context. For example, in Latin America this paradigm explains why we train others to combat illicit trafficking in South America, Central America and the Caribbean, as an effort to enable partners to provide an in-depth defence against transnational crime ranging from production areas, through transit zones, to consumption countries. In the best of cases it would be impossible for the United States, or any other single country, to be everywhere and do everything. Therefore, when we train we enable others and by doing so we achieve a multiplying effect resulting in layers of partner countries that can help stop a common enemy (i.e., traffickers of all kinds).

We also train others to help train ourselves. US special operators remain the best trainers in the world as they make use of their language skills, cultural understanding, regional knowledge and tactical proficiency. Importantly though, training others in foreign lands provides a fantastic training ground for US SOF that cannot be duplicated back home. For example, most of us could easily explain a training exercise in our first language to individuals who share a similar cultural background. This simple task becomes difficult when working in a different language and training people from a foreign culture. Nonetheless, our special operators know first-hand the great feeling of arriving at a deployed location, meeting your counterpart and being able to speak to him/her in his/her language right away. Despite the challenges of training in a foreign environment, this activity places SOF in an area where they are very adept: operating as warrior-diplomats and exercising their legendary and hard earned reputation for working by, with and through indigenous populations. The repeated exposure that special operators gain when working in foreign environments helps to build a level of comfort and proficiency in this area.

Indeed, the core of building global partnerships rests in US SOF's exceptional skills to train others. In fact, this challenging aspect of building global partnerships is what we do better than anyone else and has proven to be vitally important. We are talking about simple training events that have significant strategic impact and often represent the only acceptable US military presence in a given country. Along the spectrum of activities, we can train basic tactical skills, logistics, medical, and communications, to task force level training, for example.

Notably, the name of the game is building partner nation capacity and working with others, to include our inter-agency partners. Just like in any other endeavour, training is not devoid of politics. We train others best with SOF when the mission calls for a discreet, low visibility and logistically feasible way of achieving a desired result. With the ability to configure the force for the mission, small SOF teams often prove to be the politically acceptable solution and, with a reputation earned after decades of work in countries around the world, an easy sell for decision-makers.

SOF can normally get there faster than anyone else, and are self-sufficient and ready to go to work. Indeed, our history is replete with examples of successful training efforts: Vietnam, which shaped training advisory and training efforts for years after the war ended; Bolivia and the training that led to the capture of Che Guevara; training efforts in Colombia to help them defeat the FARC insurgency; in Iraq with the establishment of the SOF Brigade; El Salvador, training and advising the brigades and battalions that fought the Farabundo Martí National Liberation Front insurgency; and Afghanistan, where training efforts have been ongoing and likely to continue for the foreseeable future. As we continue to be engaged in combat after a decade of conflict, we have had to adjust from conducting training missions in friendly, benign situations, to training in combat. In Iraq units could be training somewhere and not to far away also engaging the enemy on active combat.

Beyond combat, training remains the logical next step everywhere we go. We fight, we enable partners (i.e., train – equip – fund – support), then we leave. Some would say that this paradigm is the new American way of war. In this context, the nation will continue to rely on USSOCOM's ability to execute its counter-terrorism role as well as Foreign Internal Defense and Unconventional Warfare (UW), among other tasks.

Key things to remember in this process are: patience; persistence; and presence. We must continue to value cultural understanding, language, and knowledge of the region, sharing our knowledge and experience, and developing long-standing relationships. Through the years we have made lasting friendships with people we have met in training deployments. If we want to understand the complexities of the region, then we have to start with building bridges of cooperation and mutual trust. We all must make it a priority to foster and promote military partnerships with our neighbours as another tool to enhance security and promote stability. For example, as the Special Operations Command (South) (SOCSOUTH) commander, I frequently met people who still remembered SOF operators they had worked with years before during training deployments and who had left such a lasting positive impression that they never forgot their names. You build these bridges one person at a time. It is not uncommon for some of these friends to become the commander of that country's Army, Navy, Air Force or Special Operations unit.

These relationships are not easy to build, however, and there are of course challenges in training others. This is a resource intensive way of doing business because we have to prepare hundreds of teams to deploy, get them there, support them, and recover back to home station. Prior to 11 September 2001 we took great pride in the amount of teams we had all over the world. Since then, wars in Iraq and Afghanistan have taken forces away from this task. We have paid the price and it will take a long time to regain the ground lost.

Additionally, in many places we have had to do more with less. USSOCOM recognizes this fact and it is constantly reviewing and adjusting engagement efforts. The most important activity we engage in is training others. If we do not pay attention to it, we will erode our hard won capability. We will lose our edge, our ability to go somewhere, gain and maintain rapport and make a difference.

While things are changing, not all changes are necessarily bad. I remember a time when we trained soldiers who had seen more combat than us in places like El Salvador and Colombia. We do not have that issue anymore. Now our friends, particularly in the Latin American region, want us to share what we have learned during the last eleven years of combat, they want to learn how to organize in joint task forces like we do. For example, in 2009 in SOCSOUTH we ran an exercise in Chile we called "Southern Star". The training vehicle was a multi-national, Combined Joint Special Operations Task Force composed of Paraguay, Uruguay, Brazil, the United States and Chile. Notably, the Brazilians, who ultimately did participate, had not initially asked the Chileans who were the hosts. The commander of the Chilean Special Operations Brigade, and my good friend, was not planning on inviting them. I also knew the commander of the Brazilian Special Operations Brigade, another good friend. Through these personal connections, I asked the Chileans to invite the Brazilians and we had a much better exercise as a result. My point is that training brings friends together more than anything else. We can disagree about many other things but we can almost always find a way to train together. As we re-set the force after adjustments in Afghanistan and Iraq, we need to get our teams out there to train others and continue to build those personal relationships. Not only do we have training skills, but we also have strong combat skills that simply underscore our abilities as trainers.

It is also important to deal with the expectations management challenge. We think we know best what our partners need and we often do not even ask them what skills they are hoping to improve. Moreover, we are used to showing up with everything to train: people, ammunition, equipment, funds. Particularly in this financial climate, we need our partners to apply some resources as well and we need to focus on specific requirements. As the demand for SOF increases, this streamlining will become increasingly more important.

Part of the solution is to recognize that training iterations seldom offer enough time to get to the level we would like and because we cannot be everywhere at once, we often lose what we gain by the time we go back. We must remember that we should train others to an achievable level, in a manner that works for the partner unit. Sometimes our standard is not the right one for them.

As a matter of strategy, it is difficult at times to tie training efforts to regional combatant command engagement strategies, especially when there is increased demand to show proof that efforts, resources, and money spent are producing measurable results. The push to show "what have you done for me lately" runs counter to the benefits of shaping the region by maintaining a steady presence. A steady presence gives the commander ground truth, eyes and ears and often the lead element when you respond to disasters. Recent examples in Latin America, such as Haiti and Guatemala, highlight this point. When Guatemala had the eruption of the Pacaya volcano, followed by torrential rains, the country was virtually isolated and U.S. Southern Command (SOUTHCOM) needed to get teams to scout out the country to assess the damage. SOCSOUTH had a Special Forces team and a naval special warfare element on the ground. They were in place and with the right connections to provide an early assessment capability until the airport could reopen. In Haiti, US Air Force Special Operations Command elements opened the airport in Port au Prince, kept it open for about a month, handled thousands of flights in and out of the country, lead on the initial efforts to evacuate people and were the first SOF command and control element on the ground. Afterwards SOF elements, comprised of Special Forces and Civil Affairs personnel, deployed throughout the country to assess damage, identify requirements, make contact with local authorities and provide visibility to the Joint Task Force commander beyond the limits of Port au Prince.

In order to have this capacity, not only do forces need to be already on the ground, training events should be synchronized with other US government activities in the host nation. For example, we should coordinate deployments so they build upon the last iteration. It could be a small engine repair mobile training team (MTT), followed by a riverine techniques mission, followed by a small unit tactical training team. Alternatively, it could be a humanitarian/civil affairs mission, followed by seminars and planning conferences. These are the building blocks for a long-term, productive engagement strategy.

We should also more critically examine which host nation elements we should engage with. We should look for those units with capability and willingness to do the job, while supporting stated goals and requirements. We tend to gravitate to units that we like regardless of whether or not they can contribute to the strategy. We must remember, however, that the best unit to train may not be a military unit. With the proper authorities the partner of choice may be a police or border patrol unit. We must also remember that any unit we train with must be vetted by the State Department to avoid assisting units with negative human rights records.

The need for partner nation engagement in order to develop capability among our friends, in short training others, has been important for a long time. Today it is more important than ever before. Whether we train in a combat area or a benign, permissive environment, the objective is still the same: training and enabling others builds and gives others the opportunity to be full partners in shaping the security environment. As we contemplate a future beyond Iraq and Afghanistan, training others, building partner nation capacity and re-establishing our presence in the world, will be key to maintaining peace and a safe and secure environment.

CHAPTER 5

THE CANADIAN SPECIAL OPERATIONS REGIMENT: THE DDMA EXPERIENCE

LIEUTENANT-COLONEL JOHN VASS

This chapter explores the Canadian Special Operations Regiment's (CSOR) recent history with tasks associated with Defence, Development and Military Assistance operations. In particular, CSOR experiences in Afghanistan, Jamaica and Africa are examined. Importantly, while CSOR might be a relatively new asset to help the Government of Canada achieve DDMA tasks, and while DDMA might be a new title, providing specialized military advice, training and assistance is not a new endeavour for western militaries.

In the American lexicon, Foreign Internal Defense and, more recently, SFA operations refer to missions designed to asses, train, advise and assist host nation (HN) military and paramilitary forces with operations designed to enhance their ability to provide security within their borders. Quite simply, the objective is to enable these forces to maintain the HN's internal stability, to counter subversion and violence in their country, and to address the causes of instability. These missions, specifically SFA, also include a focus on population security by providing supervision of tactical operations conducted by HN military units to neutralize and destroy insurgent threats, isolate insurgents from the civil population, and protect the civil population.[1]

In addition, military forces may be assigned the responsibility for police training and must be prepared to assume that role if required.[2] Again, these training tasks are often followed by the conduct of operations in support of these forces. Preferably, the police or military force is trained, equipped and mentored into an organized unit prior to executing joint operations; however, this timeline is not always possible and often coalition forces are required to act in support of HN forces that have a minimal level of training and insufficient equipment.

Using recent Canadian terminology, DDMA operations, similar to FID/SFA operations, contribute to nation-building through support to select states through the provision of specialized military advice, training and assistance. In the Canadian context, particularly with respect to CANSOFCOM, military assistance focuses on DFAIT sponsored countries and programs. Other than CSOR's efforts in Afghanistan, their Special Forces (SF) Teams[3] typically deploy in support of DFAIT's Counter Terrorism Capacity Building Program and focus their efforts on military capacity building, infrastructure advice and expertise, equipment recommendations, procurement assistance, and training assistance.[4]

As mentioned, this chapter will discuss CSOR's experience in conducting DDMA type operations in Afghanistan, Jamaica and Africa. After defining the central task for each operation, the discussion will focus on the effects and results achieved by each team, followed by a summary of lessons learned. Notably, the information in this chapter is reflective of the thoughts, opinions and observations of the author gained through his experience as the commanding officer responsible for the force generation of the SF Teams deployed in these roles. Additionally, for operational security reasons, certain details will be omitted.

AFGHANISTAN

CSOR participated in various training missions as part of their commitment to the CANSOFCOM SOTF under the construct of Joint Task Force – Afghanistan. As the situation in Kandahar province changed, so did their various partnered forces. CSOR's niche was initially carved out with elements of the United States Special

Forces (USSF) training initiative of the ANA Commando initiative, which saw a training team embedded in the Commando Training Program. However, once the assigned Afghan Commando element was redeployed elsewhere in Afghanistan, CSOR focused initially on an ANA reconnaissance platoon, subsequently followed by the creation of the Provincial Response Company (PRC), while concurrently, they trained local security elements as part of a Village Stability Operation. With the withdrawal of Canadian forces from Kandahar province in 2011, CSOR is now participating in the training and mentorship of ANA Special Operations Forces in Kabul as part of the Canadian Contribution Training Mission – Afghanistan (CCTM-A).

ANA COMMANDO TRAINING

The ANA Commando Program provided the fertilizer for the growth of CSOR training assistance and cooperation operations. With humble beginnings as embeds with the USSF, CSOR operators soon established themselves as world-class trainers, which included numerous successful partnered operations against insurgent forces throughout Kandahar province. This line of operation provided our operators with exceptional operational mentorship experience and offered an opportunity to deepen our relations with both our USSF counterparts and the ANA.

With the redeployment of our assigned Afghan Commando element, members of the Canadian Special Operations Forces (CANSOF) SOTF began negotiations to establish a partnered force that could be used for their own operations, specifically as "the Afghan face" to missions as part of the process of training and handing over responsibility for security operations to the ANSF. With concurrence from the senior leadership of the ANA, members of an ANA reconnaissance (recce) platoon were tasked as a partnered force for the Canadians. This was the birth of the self-proclaimed ANA TOOFAN (Storm Troopers).

ANA TOOFAN (STORM TROOPERS)

The force generation of the TOOFAN was primarily based on elements from an ANA recce platoon. With thorough and detailed instruction in basic and advanced soldiering skills, the highly motivated members of the TOOFAN were transformed into a competent and reliable partnered force to support SOTF operations. More importantly though, the TOOFAN deepened their effectiveness to the point where they were capably conducting very successful independent operations.

Nonetheless, with the re-deployment of their parent organization elsewhere in Afghanistan, the Storm Troopers also relocated thereby leaving the CANSOF SOTF without a partner force once again. As a result, the CANSOF SOTF negotiated with the HN and struck a deal with the ANP. As a result, the CANSOF SOTF agreed to provide training to a group of police officers in order to create a PRC which would be capable of acting as a partner force for SOTF operations.

ANP – PRC

The creation of the ANP PRC was a definite success story that saw a relatively inexperienced, poorly trained and equipped group of Afghan police transformed into a cohesive unit. With the candidates having a police background, the training focused on basic and advanced soldiering skills ranging from marksmanship and tactical driving, to combat first aid and basic police skills that, notably, were taught by members of the Royal Canadian Mounted Police. Their growth and maturity as an effective unit was impressive and was showcased during the Siege on Kandahar. Indeed, while the PRC provided a partner force for the SOTF, more importantly, it conducted independent operations and became the force of choice of the Afghan Ministry of Interior (MoI).

For example, in early May 2011, during a significant insurgent attack on Kandahar, the PRC answered the call and their performance showcased the well-deserved trust and reliance that the Government of Afghanistan had in their abilities. With the Governor's palace under siege, the Afghan MoI initiated the employment of the PRC, which in turn deployed elements independently from the CANSOF SOTF base outside Kandahar City. Importantly, the PRC defeated a number of insurgents in the outlying buildings and secured the palace compound area. When additional attacks came from neighboring buildings, the remainder of the PRC deployed with its CSOR mentors. The battle ensued until the early morning hours. The PRC's rapid deployment and successful resolution of the incident provided a superb demonstration of their ability and proved that they were aptly the force of choice against a determined and unrelenting enemy.

After showcasing their capabilities and perseverance, upon redeployment back to their forward operating base early that morning, the PRC received yet another warning order to resolve another incident in the Kandahar City area. This time it was a coordinated insurgent attack on a prominent Kandahar hotel. After a deliberate planning cycle, the PRC deployed to the incident site. However, upon arrival, other ANP elements had the situation already resolved. Nonetheless, the PRC had solidified their reputation as a rapidly deployable force of choice that could be relied upon by the Government of Afghanistan.[5] Notably, with the withdrawal of Canadian forces from Kandahar, the PRC was partnered with Allied Forces to continue their efforts in bringing security and stability to the citizens of Kandahar.

VSO

Canadian Special Forces were also involved in village stability operations that represented a joint program with the USSF, which involved a Canadian SF Team partnered with elements of the Afghan National Civil Order Police. The program was designed to establish security, governance and development at the village level by recruiting and training local forces in security operations.

The Canadian efforts, along with their partnered force, were responsible for contributing to the preliminary re-establishment of district governance at the local level. Their numerous operations created a disruptive effect on insurgent networks within their area of operations and also gave CSOR operators an excellent venue to develop their ability to conduct independent operations, which had a lasting positive effect on the village and an equally lasting negative effect on insurgents. This particular line of operation was critical in exposing members of our young Regiment to irregular warfare. Similar to the PRC, the withdrawal of Canadian forces from the Kandahar region saw their partnered force working with other members of the coalition force. Nonetheless, for the VSO operations CSOR operators deployed to the Kabul area as part of the CCTM – A.

CCTM – A

As of 2012, CSOR personnel are employed by the Special Operations Advisory Group under the construct of the National Training Mission – Afghanistan. Specifically, CSOR operators provide staff mentorship to ANA Special Operations Command (ANASOC) and, as instructors on their qualification course, contribute to the grass roots training of ANA Special Operations Forces. While not employed in operational mentorship roles, their efforts will indirectly contribute to the security of the Afghan people. Additionally, their presence will continue to deepen our relations with our allies and enhance our operators' capabilities in conducting training assistance missions.

Unquestionably, the professionalism of CSOR operators is having a lasting effect as the ANA grows its SOF capability. Moreover, there is no doubt that they have contributed to the successful development of certain elements of the ANP.

JAMAICA

In addition to their efforts in Afghanistan, CSOR also has an enduring relationship with elements of the Jamaica Defence Force (JDF). As part of the DFAIT's Counter Terrorism Capacity Building Program, CSOR has developed an enduring relationship with the CT elements of the JDF.

CSOR's first deployment to Jamaica in 2008, represented the Regiment's inaugural DDMA mission outside of a mature theatre of operations. The program is closely synchronized with other allied efforts and the operational cycle of the JDF. This is strictly a training and mentoring task with no operational employment on the part of Canadian Forces members.

Notably, the JDF has conducted numerous successful operations in their country. Nonetheless, based on lessons learned from these missions, CSOR members help identify gaps in their skills and assist in providing the necessary training. The objectives of these training missions are to help build the JDF capacity to conduct CT operations, enhance its ability to enforce the domestic rule-of-law, to build and maintain professional relationships between the Canadian Forces and the JDF, and to act as a technical advisor for equipment procurement and infrastructure development.

This particular mission represents a significant success story as CSOR members continue to build their capability in conducting training tasks while our JDF partners expertly refine their skills. Importantly, the lessons learned by the Regiment through all phases of the training mission from warning, preparation and training, deployment, employment all the way to redeployment have all been successfully integrated into follow-on engagements in Africa. In fact, the program now serves as a template for further global engagements.

AFRICA

In support of the Canadian Counter Terrorism Capacity Building Program and the US Special Operations Command – Africa (SOC Africa), specifically, Joint Special Operations Task Force – Trans Sahal efforts, CSOR SF Teams are participating in the training and mentorship of Malian Security Forces (MSF). While MSF are engaged in active operations, Canadian elements are not playing an operational mentorship role. Instead, CSOR's focus remains on training. With its focus on helping the Malians to build their capacity to conduct CT operations, building and maintaining a professional relationship and acting as technical advisors for equipment procurement and infrastructure development, the operation is a success. Specifically, the Regiment continues to deepen its training capability, gain exposure to a new environment, build relationships with our African partners and deepen our ties with US and other allied Special Forces.

SUMMARY

While FID, SFA and DDMA are not new concepts, CSOR is relatively new to the community that typically conducts these activities. Through lessons learned on each mission, the Regiment continues to deepen its capability and refine its skill-sets. As such, it is important to examine the lessons learned thus far.

LESSONS LEARNED

CSOR's lessons learned range from a tactical to a strategic level of operations and each lesson has assisted the Regiment in deepening its capability in conducting DDMA. While not an exhaustive list, some critical lessons identified through discussions with CSOR's Regimental Operations Officer are outlined below:

1. It is important to build and employ operationally self-sufficient teams. Without the appropriate combat support and combat service support our operators cannot successfully execute their tasks. Ranging from diplomatic clearances to the movement of equipment on military aircraft, we need trained personnel to be effective. With very limited resources, surging support elements forward, as required, provides an efficient and economical means to support a team.

2. DDMA tasks require long-term commitment. Not only is there a significant staff effort required to set up a program but, equally important, if we truly want our partnered force to progress, a close, long-lasting, relationship is required. This commitment will allow our partnered force to develop ownership in the development and proficiency of skills, which will have the twofold effect of deepening their pride in their capabilities while also reinforcing our commitment to them and the program.

3. Cultural awareness and language capabilities are critical. Extensive cultural/regional understanding provides context for operations and helps to establish credibility for our forces. The ability to communicate with indigenous partnered forces represents a huge advantage; however, with limited human resources, building an agile, responsive and effective operational language capability and cultural understanding is a significant challenge. At a minimum, to harness the cultural awareness of a particular country, SF Teams must continue to build and disseminate institutional theatre knowledge.

4. It is important to select the appropriate HN partnered force. This process will clearly have a significant influence on achieving a desired effect and enable the team to assist in creating a regional impact. A thorough analysis and understanding of HN dynamics prior to operations is critical as the partnered force will develop lethal skill-sets.

5. <u>It is important to select the appropriate approach to training</u>. In this context, there are two approaches to training: institutional and instructional. The institutional approach means the HN delivers the training to its own forces. As a result, the end result may take a bit longer as it is necessary to build a training cadre with experience that can expertly train others. As such, the HN makes a deliberate choice to give up immediate short-term outcomes by not using an external training team that could deliver the necessary training quickly and effectively. However, it trades immediate results for longer term capability (i.e. an approach that sees the outcome more in line as a marathon rather than a sprint).

The instructional approach sees the delivery of a focused and intensive training package to a HN. Experience has proven that for the instructional approach to have a desired effect, persistent engagement is necessary and without it apparent gains are fragile. Finding the sweet-spot in the approach to training is always a challenge but we are finding that a natural evolution from instructional to institutional training is effective providing there is a long-term commitment to the HN.

6. <u>Formal training requirements (individual and collective) are necessary for the SOF Team</u>. While the level of training of our operators is extremely high, certain specialist requirements exist and the challenge is finding a sustainable solution to either augment a team with the required specialists or to train the operators to a standard that they can execute the tasks on their own. In order to keep their skill-sets at a high level, we continue to develop ways to deepen their skills without expanding them to a degree that is impractical to maintain. As technology moves forward in communications, equipment and finances, so do the training requirements to manage them. As a result,

although always conscious of how other SOF organizations conduct operations and resource themselves, it is important to understand the realities and limitations of your own organization. As such, for CSOR, the answer is surging specialists forward to the point of need when required rather than trying to make everyone an expert in everything.

7. Joint, Interagency, Multinational and Public awareness is necessary. This aspect of our SF Teams is critical to the success of the mission as their tactical efforts on the ground typically have strategic effects. Their ability to operate and coordinate effectively with other government departments and agencies (OGD/A) of Canada, allied countries and the host nations is a skill-set that our team members must be advised on, with experience allowing them to perfect these communication skills. Equally important, as representatives of the Government of Canada with a specific mission to accomplish, our SF Teams must also have the requisite authorities to liaison with the requisite partner and HN forces prior to deployment, as well as the flexibility to adjust their plan as the mission progresses.

8. One should never underestimate the value of a well-timed demonstration. Through experience, we have found that HNs are sometimes hesitant to employ their forces in critical roles. Coordinating a thoroughly rehearsed demonstration of capabilities provides an excellent opportunity to showcase the partnered force. In some cases strategic decisions about the operational employment of the HN force are based on their impressions of the demonstration. Equally important, this process assists in achieving HN buy-in to leverage limited indigenous resources.[6]

CONCLUSION

This chapter explored CSOR's experience in conducting DDMA type operations in Afghanistan, Jamaica and Africa over the course of an approximately five-year period. While the concepts of DDMA are not necessarily new, the Regiment is relatively young and will continue to hone its skills through the execution of these missions and harnessing the experience gained by our allies and those of the forces we train.

NOTES

1   Department of the Army, *FM 3-05, Counterinsurgency* (Washington, DC: Government Printing Office, December 2006), 2-2.

2   Ibid., 6-20.

3   SF in this case refers to CANSOF elements, specifically from CSOR, who train indigenous forces.

4   Notably, CSOR's contributions are managed within their areas of expertise.

5   Discussion with Green Team Leader responsible for Training the PRC dated 1 Nov 2011.

6   Discussions with CSOR Operations Officer dated 1 Nov 2011.

CHAPTER 6

THE ACID TEST OF REALITY: ACCOUNTS OF WORKING WITH OTHERS FROM THE FRONT LINES IN IRAQ AND AFGHANISTAN

DR. BILL KNARR

Do not try to do too much with your own hands. Better the Arabs do it tolerably than that you do it perfectly. It is their war, and you are to help them, not to win it for them.[1]

T.E Lawrence

Although T.E. Lawrence spoke of working with Arabs to help them fight their war, his comment is relevant when working with any people or population expected to assume responsibility for their own security – Iraqi, Afghan, Haitian, Bosnian and Colombian, for example. US Secretary of Defense Robert Gates presented the 2007 version of Lawrence's truism as, "the most important military component in the War on Terror[ism] is not the fighting we do ourselves, but how well we enable and empower our partners to defend and govern themselves."[2] In addition to being strategically and operationally smart, it is also economically imperative as we look towards partnerships and cost-sharing to achieve our security objectives.[3]

The purpose of this chapter is to provide the views of operators who have experience "working with others."[4] This chapter is based on a panel discussion which consisted of four special operations forces operators, two Americans and two Canadians, with recent field experience, which was held at the *SOF: Building Global Partnerships* symposium.

The US contribution comprised US Master Chief Troy Ivie and US Sergeant Major Randy Krueger. Master Chief Troy Ivie, Sea-Air-Land (SEAL) is from the Center for SEAL and the Special Warfare Center in California. Master Chief Ivie enlisted in the Navy in 1984 and graduated from Basic Underwater Demolition School in 1990. He served with SEAL teams in Southern, European and Central Commands' areas of operation to include operations in Central and South America, the Balkans, Africa, and Iraq. Sergeant Major Randy Krueger, Special Forces, is currently the Operations Sergeant Major with the Special Forces Command, Fort Bragg, North Carolina. Sergeant Major Krueger entered the Army in 1985 and completed the Special Forces Qualification Course in 1993. From 1993 to 2000 he served with the 7th Special Forces Group and deployed to Central and South America with various operational detachments. Krueger's combat deployments include Desert Storm and four tours to Operation Enduring Freedom.

The two Canadian participants were Sergeant Patrick Twomey and Major David Suffoletta. Sergeant Patrick Twomey, Detachment Commander 1, CSOR, is a founding member of CSOR and completed the Special Operations Qualification Course in 2007. His DDMA operational experience includes Bosnia in 2003, Afghanistan in 2008 and 2010 and Jamaica in 2011. As part of those deployments to Afghanistan he was Strike Detachment Commander on exchange with United States Special Forces Operational Detachment Alpha (ODA) 3131 in Khakrez, Kandahar Province. He was also the Chief Instructor for the stand-up of the first platoon of the Afghan National Police Provincial Response Company – Kandahar (PRC-K). Major David Suffoletta, a member of CSOR, deployed with the last Canadian Special Operation Task Force to Afghanistan prior to the cessation of Canadian combat operations in Kandahar. His team was responsible for developing and mentoring the PRC-K. The PRC Kandahar is an ISAF SOF program. They are part of the Afghan National Police and fall under the Afghan Minister of Interior.

During the panel, the operators discussed experiences and lessons, both positive and negative, which arose when working with other militaries, particularly with regard to training missions in Iraq and Afghanistan. Each of the four operator perspectives that are outlined below underscores the uniqueness of their experiences. Nonetheless, there are common threads. In particular, the importance of understanding culture was highlighted by each participant, as were the challenges of linking tactical actions to the expressed strategic goal and, in some cases, to a coherent exit strategy and *vice versa*. These themes will be expanded upon below. Notably, while the operators' perspectives have been grouped thematically, as much as possible, their stories have been recounted in their own words.

THE EVOLUTION OF TRAINING OTHERS

Tell me and I forget. Teach me and I remember. Involve me and I learn.

              – Benjamin Franklin[5]

It is important to note that the theme of training others, often prevalent under the SOF tasking of Forward Internal Defense, now more commonly SFA in the US and DDMA in Canada is not a recent phenomenon. In fact, one operator noted that he had over 20 years of experience in training others as part of the US Navy SEALs.

Having worked extensively in Central America, Europe, and most recently in Iraq, Master Chief Ivie has witnessed first hand the evolution of partnership training and cultural exchanges and suggested that 9/11 marked a turning point in the focus of these activities. Pre-9/11 he noted that training focused on "regional, long-term development with our partners." As Ivie continued, "the enemy was common to both the training force and the mentored force and was a very visible person that we trained to fight against. We spent [a lot of] time in the field training with our partners. We shared tradecraft. We shared our [military] cultures."

Post 9/11, however, some things changed. As Ivie remarked, now "it is much more battle-focused. In the past, we deployed for presence. In this day and age we deploy more for purpose, to go and do a particular job." Ivie continued to explain that today's "intelligence based, battle focused training," occurs in "an asymmetric, urban environment, with particular mission sets." The important distinction, he commented, is that "the enemy is no longer external. The enemy could be in the room, and in some cases he was in Iraq, sitting there in the room with us. That is what we face today – an enemy that lives in those seams of what we call good law enforcement, what we call counterinsurgency, what we call counterterrorism. He purposely lives in those seams. That's the enemy we face, and the enemy we now train our partners to understand."

Nonetheless, Master Chief Ivie also emphasized that while some things changed post 9/11, some things remained the same. He observed that "what has not changed is how we approach [training] and how we teach those guys, face-to-face." He also noted that this practice is particular to SOF. As he explained, "We [SOF] live with them, eat with them, we sleep with them, we fight with them."

While Master Chief Ivie spoke of training others, SFA and FID are also commonly referred to as training missions. Notably, in this context, training is much broader than what most people would typically visualize. For those that would discriminate among terms, these operators are also teachers, coaches, mentors and partners who must depend on each other in life and death situations. As such, they must know when, where and how to apply their various skills.[6] In order to do so effectively, they must be able to work in various cultural contexts.

CULTURE

Culture defined as "a shared set of traditions, belief systems, and behaviours...." was a common-denominator as the operators frequently cited cultural characteristics that impacted their ability to train partnership forces.[7] In fact, the operators quickly learned that cultural beliefs and values shaped not only how locals behaved but also how their own behaviours were interpreted.

Importantly, it soon became evident that how textbooks describe culture and how people actually live are not always the same. For instance, most people have likely heard that an Afghan's identity and loyalty lies in his family, clan, tribe and so on and while that may, in general terms, be true, operators have tested that theory and the adherence to *Pashtunwali*, the Pashtun code of behaviour, and have sometimes been astonished by the results. For example, Sergeant Major Krueger described his surprise as he tried to determine the ethnicity of Afghan Commandos in the Kabul Airport awaiting transport to Kandahar. He explained, "I was trying to get to know the culture better and as the soldiers were coming through and I said, 'Hey you look like you are Pashtun, where are you from?' or, 'You look like you are Hazara, are you from Niley, are you from Herat, where are you from?' Their response was, 'I'm an Afghan; I'm a Commando.'" Krueger realized that "they took pride in the fact they were Commandos and different than the regular forces. They identified with Afghanistan, not necessarily just with their own tribe." Krueger was pleasantly taken by this realization. He noted that "trying to get them linked back to their tribe was important, and even a connection to their ethnic background was important, but it was more important to link them to the bigger picture of Afghanistan, to take ownership of security of their own country."

Sergeant Twomey also had a personal account that serves as a salient reminder that academic studies are never a substitute for ground truth. He explained, "I studied the Pashtun code of honour, *Pashtunwali*, and Afghan history but once on the ground I soon realized things were much different where I was. Many of the areas we operated were ripped apart by conflict and much of the cultural fabric had been torn and so they did not necessarily know or subscribe to *Pashtunwali*."

Another cultural challenge that the operators faced was the apparent contradictions that exist in some cultures. For example, Master Chief Ivie discussed the confusion he faced regarding the Iraqi honour system and honesty in that culture. He explained, "It's the culture of an honour system to the point of not being honest with you in order to protect their honour."

Master Chief Ivie also noted that issues such as military maintenance – or the lack there of – could also be attributed to different cultural beliefs and values. He commented, "To this day it's hard to get [Iraqis] to understand that if you don't put oil in the HMMWV [High Mobility Multipurpose Wheeled Vehicle] months on end, the engine is going to eventually blow up. Or if you don't stock oil on the shelves you won't have any oil to put in the trucks. So it's that culture that we fought every day there."

Using History to Achieve Objectives

While cultural differences could present challenges, they could also provide a rich source of inspiration. Sergeant Twomey provided an example from his experience in working with the Afghan Provincial Response Company in 2010 of how history and culture can be used to build morale in partner organizations. He cautions that you can use your own country's history as an example, but ultimately, your partner must build on their own history and traditions. Twomey explained:

> During training, the Provincial Response Company began to complain about the quality of their equipment, and demanding more. At one point I sat them down and told them about the Second Battle of Ypres, when the German army released choking chlorine gas during an attack and virtually every army fled before the poisonous clouds.

Every unit except the Canadians, who held the line despite having no proper equipment to protect themselves against the gas, who improvised by holding urine soaked rags to their mouths to filter out the fumes and fought back, ultimately defeating the German attack.

I then compared this example with that of the Mujahedeen, who first fought back against the invading Soviets with ancient bolt-action rifles. All they needed was their rifle, and the heart of a warrior. After that the complaints for better equipment dropped off dramatically. What is important to note is that within the appeal to the better part of their nature, there is a touch of shaming, but mostly it is about instilling in them a sense of pride of being the latest in a line of brave warriors.

Leading by Example

Another way that the cultural chasm could be bridged was through leading by example. Each of the operators in one form or another suggested that leading by example and living among the people they were helping to protect and train contributed to successful missions. As Master Chief Ivie noted of his time in Iraq, "we live with them, we eat with them, we sleep with them, we fight with them." Indeed, in Afghanistan, one of the basic principles of the VSO program is that "Living in the Village is what sets us apart from all other forces...Your team should live among the people."[8]

In addition to living with local forces, it was important to be hands-on when leading training exercises rather that to just sit back and watch the local force practice. As Sergeant Twomey put it, "Never explain what you can demonstrate." In addition to being instructional it was one of the best means of communications. Twomey continued, "This was important for many reasons; not least of which was the language barrier when instructing students whose language you do not speak." Nonetheless, although he advocated leading by example he cautioned, "You must also be hyper-aware of the example you are setting. Related to never explaining what you can demonstrate, asking villagers to help you protect them from the Taliban by informing on them demonstrates where your interests really lie, in your own protection and not theirs. The reality is all they have to do to protect themselves is to keep their mouths shut and countenance minimal contact with you." He continued, "do not think that it does not pass notice that Taliban cells that target coalition forces are dealt with swiftly, while those that target the people are hardly dealt with at all. One of the Village Stability Platform keystone documents on methodology perhaps put it best, 'you must protect the population as if your mission and your life depend on it.'"[9]

Although leading by example and living in their reality is primarily about human interactions, equipping partners also had its place in building strong relationships. Sergeant Major Krueger explained:

> One of the lessons learned is that if you outfitted them with better equipment, they were a lot more effective. As an example, it was not helpful to have an American out there with an M-4, M-16 rifle with cool optics and lasers and wearing NVGs [night vision goggles] while these guys come up in flop flops and a rusty AK-47. They may have a helmet if they haven't sold it at the bazaar to make a little extra money for their family. But if you showed up with those cool things, it said, "Hey, look what I've got that you can't have." We found it was a deterrent to training and to making them an effective force.

It's All About Behaviour

At the end of the day, as Sergeant Twomey noted, "It's all about behaviour, especially when you are training partner forces." As they prepared to standup the Provincial Response Company,

Sergeant Twomey recalled an After Action Report comment from a Coalition partner unit that had stood-up a PRC in a neighbouring province. It read in part, "Honesty and integrity are not ANP traits. If you leave anything lying around, expect it to get stolen, if you lend them something don't expect to get it back." This comment was not considered unusual nor was the information considered novel. In fact, these critiques were already firmly part of the ANP's reputation. This expression of ANP culture is what Sergeant Twomey considered to be his real challenge. In the end, he commented, "the majority of the training that we do, teaching them how to shoot, move, and communicate, is fairly straightforward. Honesty and integrity are a much bigger challenge and training a negative or the absence of certain specified behaviours can be much more difficult."

That was not the only challenge, however. They had four weeks to prepare the PRC for Initial Operating Capability, so time and keeping them focused and motivated as they fast-paced through the course were also critical. According to Sergeant Twomey, in addition to the standard courses on tactics and marksmanship his team also "informally identified the desirable and undesirable behaviours we needed to respectively promote and extinguish. When it came to [dealing with issues of] honesty and integrity, we mostly focused on discouraging and dealing with theft. When it came to promoting honesty and integrity we just had to hope to recognize it when we saw it."

As in his approach to dealing with the different villages in working Village Stability Operations with ODA 3131, the next step after identifying the desirable and undesirable behaviours, was to identify the "currency" that the target audience coveted. Twomey elaborated, "every day I would identify certain behaviours that I observed in the candidates, and we would have our 'Heroes of the Day' where individuals would come up front to be recognized and receive a round of applause from their peers. Their response was overwhelmingly positive." He continued, "as an example on one of the first days I recognized the best shooters, and then the next day on the range everyone who shot half-decently had to show us their target and wanted us to write their name down."

Notably, though while identifying and reinforcing skill-sets was relatively easy, the real challenge remained dealing with issues of honesty and integrity. Then a situation arose that provided a giant step forward for the team in this regard. As Twomey explained:

> One of the candidates had a negligent discharge on the range; shooting after the cease-fire order (in Pashto) was given. Unusually, he quickly admitted his fault and apologized, promising it would never happen again. This made him the big 'Hero of the Day' for his display of honesty and integrity. I emphasized that although he was still getting a red chit for this transgression, the end result was that I now trusted him more than before. I cannot trust someone to correct a mistake that they do not admit making in the first place. His honesty was also exemplary of the type of behaviour that should be expected...

The inaugural PRC course ended on time and with, according to Twomey, an "impressive live fire demonstration encompassing virtually all the skills they were taught." But what was more gratifying was an incident that occurred shortly before that. As Twomey explained,

> One morning I arrived at the PRC lines to issue out their weapons when one of the candidates approached me to return the pen I had dropped out of the HMMWV as I had driven away the previous night. That one simple act, more than anything else we did during the IOC [Initial Operational Capability] demonstration upon their graduation, showed the success of our efforts to build a culture of honesty and integrity, and the potential we had with the PRC-K.

Nonetheless, as leaders look for those incentives, Sergeant Twomey cautions that they need to be constantly curious about motives, because motives are different from one village to the next. Once again referring back to the Village Stability Platform keystone documents he noted, "if you've seen one VSO, you've seen one VSO."[10]

Know and Learn From Your Enemy

Sun Tzu's famous quote, "if you know yourself and you know your enemy you need not fear," came to mind as the operators discussed enemy tactics, capabilities and intelligence. In fact, they took it one step further underscoring the point that one can learn valuable lessons by observing the enemy's behaviour. For example, it was noted that it is educational to understand how the Taliban operate and the value that the Afghan people see in their methods and operations. Sergeant Twomey cited what he described as the Taliban's streamlined and flexible structure as an example:

> While on a liaison task to Maiwand, I had the privilege to accompany an ODA team as they patrolled out of Combat Outpost (COP) Rath. While providing over watch of the foot patrol from a high feature we listened in on Taliban communications. They began with each sub-commander providing a situation report of what activities they had conducted, and any requests they had for supplies or fighters. It was then followed up by their higher commander passing on new observed coalition tactics, along with some advice on countering them. After that, the commander passed on propaganda messages to pass on to the villagers about what the infidels were there to do, and it concluded with a religious lecture.

> There was a truism in Afghanistan that if we ever did the same tactic twice the Taliban knew about it, and the third time you did it they would have adapted to it and nail you. It wasn't hard to see how. Even though their

communications were in the open, they were so quick and adaptive compared with us that we often couldn't keep up except in the most minor areas.

Sergeant Twomey also commented on some of benefits the people see in working with the Taliban and how the Coalition might use that knowledge to their advantage:

> In Afghanistan no one goes to the Taliban for medical attention or to get a water well dug. The number one service they [Taliban] provide is a court system; in many areas they are the ones people trust to adjudicate disputes. Knowing this will tell you where to place your priorities if this is what occurs in your area. For example in Khakrez it would inform us to prioritize the shaping of the water council to adjudicating disputes by carefully building up their reputation for fairness, all the better to use it as a wedge to drive out support for the Taliban in the area.

As Sergeant Twomey exhibited an in-depth understanding of Taliban operations and tactics, Master Chief Ivie discussed, in general, the importance and evolution of intelligence and intelligence support, especially as it related to training the Iraqi Security Forces and the significance of human intelligence and their networks. Ivie remarked, "I see now and in the future, more emphasis on intelligence. I see a large robust intel[ligence] picture and a smaller more agile unit taking advantage of that intelligence. Intelligence wise, I think we taught them well, that there is no better intelligence than their own networks. We taught them how to enhance that network on the ground with their resources."

DEVELOPING THE PROVINCIAL RESPONSE COMPANY[11]

The development of the Provincial Response Company provides a good case study for how all these cultural pieces fit together in practice. The PRC was part of the Afghan National Police under the Minister of Interior and was an ISAF SOF program. The intent was to stand-up a PRC in major urban areas across the country as special police with enhanced capabilities. As the ANA had the Commandos, the ANP had the PRC, which was viewed primarily as a Special Weapons and Tactics, or a SWAT-like force. It is instructive to hear the rest of the story from Major David Suffoletta's perspective as he deployed in 2011 with the last Canadian Special Operation Task Force to Afghanistan prior to the cease of Canadian combat operations in Kandahar and worked with the PRC-K.

Their missions covered everything from deliberate detention and crisis response to force protection, mobility, and other things. Major Suffoletta's team was the task force lead in developing and mentoring the PRC. That role included operational mentorship as well as training. The team encountered a number of challenges in the areas of program institutionalization and force development versus force deployment/employment.

The institutionalization of the program involved curriculum, formalized training, courseware development, qualification and standardization. The mere number of forces and nations involved in a program that was Afghanistan-wide, provides an indication of the standardization issues that needed to be addressed.

Considerable time and energy was spent in creation of NATO style training manuals, training plans, establishment of standards and granting of qualifications. With institutionalization came the challenges surrounding logistics. The ANP logistics system was cumbersome and unresponsive which led the PRC not to trust it or use it. As Major Suffoletta remarked, "We had to constantly mentor them to get them to use the system and go through the proper channels, otherwise they would go through their own channels." He explained, "Although they would be successful at getting what they wanted, this would undermine the ANP logistic system and what we were trying to achieve. So getting the PRC to use their logistics system and getting the system to respond was a constant battle."

The second major challenge was force development versus force employment. As the PRC gained credibility and capability it became more and more in demand by their own chain of command within the ANP to employ them. This was good news and bad news. While they were building the organization, they had to temper the demand for employment. As Suffoletta noted:

> We actually reached a point where we almost completely put development by the wayside because of PRC force employment tempo. We reached a tipping point. There was a week or two that they were being deployed so often we were unable to meet force development aims. Eventually we were able to push back and find a balance between force development and employment, but I'm not sure we ever found the perfect balance.

The other employment challenge was developing and adhering to an employment concept. Because of the unit's specialized training, it was viewed by the ANP leadership and some of the leaders within the PRC as a unit of first response, like a Quick Reaction Force (QRF). However, the intent was that the unit would be the force of last resort. Major Suffoletta explained, "We intended it more of a force of last resort during a crisis response. The concept is, first understand the situation, pick the instant or location where you can have max effect, and then commit them." He observed, "The ANP command viewed the PRC more as a QRF, first incident, first call, out the door as fast as they can and rush to the objective. So we continually tried to message force of last resort versus force of first choice."

There were also friction points with regard to intelligence gathering. As Suffoletta explained, "we worked with the ANP and

Coalition partners within the operational coordination centre in downtown Kandahar to try to establish a process whereby intelligence can be brought to Afghan commanders for them to make decisions and then they could task the PRC to conduct deliberate pre-emptive operations." He concluded that they had achieved limited success.

Major Suffoletta cited events of 7-9 May 2011 as an example of the challenges and successes of employing the PRC. On 7 May there were attacks throughout Kandahar city by insurgents, mostly targeting Afghan government facilities. Initially, as part of their role in crisis response, the PRC deployed on their own to a location near the Governor's compound, in downtown Kandahar. There they linked up with the Afghan Security forces in place and helped them suppress an objective from which the insurgents were attacking the Governor's compound. After awhile they moved forward with other Afghan forces to clear that objective – unassisted by the Canadians except for an emergency resupply of rocket propelled grenades.

After the first objective was cleared, the PRC was reoriented to a second objective held by insurgents just south of, and attacking, the Governor's compound. Clearance of that objective went into the night of the 7th and then paused because the PRC had suffered some casualties. It had been a long day and night time made the fighting even more difficult. The next morning they completed the mission and quickly cleared the objective.

On the morning of 9 May, the PRC was deployed to deal with the final holdout of insurgents in support of an ANSF unit, not an ANP unit, a factor that would become important later. The ANSF unit had cleared half of the objective the day before, but had stalled. As the PRC, with their Canadian SOF partners, completed their leaders' recon and pulled back to begin deliberate planning, the ANSF resumed and completed the clearing operation.

CHAPTER 6

One might ask why the ANSF resumed the operation without waiting for PRC support. Major Suffoletta offered a possible explanation:

> My assessment of this result is that after we met the in-place force during the leader's recce and they talked with the PRC command, saw some Canadian SOF supporting him and saw us all nod that the PRC could handle it from there – it kind of shamed them into starting to clear it again. The leader of the in-place ANSF didn't want the PRC and by extension the ANP to steal the honour of finishing the job.

The events of 7-9 May and the PRC's role was briefed to US General Petraeus, Commander, ISAF. Per Major Suffoletta, General Petraeus commented, "It is too bad they don't have the equivalent of the Presidential Unit Citation for Afghan Police units because that PRC down there probably deserves it." Shortly thereafter, the Afghan Minister of Interior visited Kandahar and decorated several of the PRC officers and gave the PRC commander money to help take care of their wounded.

As a result of their actions, the PRC was also developing a good reputation with the people of Kandahar, in opposition to some of the other ANSF units. A few days after the events of 7-9 May, the PRC Commander made some very interesting comments. He said that the next day when people were returning to work near the second objective, near the Governor's compound, they were happy and surprised to find all of their belongings intact. Nothing had been looted or stolen and no unnecessary damage had been done. They attributed that to the honesty and trustworthiness of the PRC.

In conclusion, Major Suffoletta offered these final thoughts on working with the PRC:

The first is when we worked on institutionalizing the PRC and having them conduct operations. Because we wanted them to be the lead but did not have the time or resources to get them to our level we had to determine what was 'good enough', but it's not easy. Especially for our operators, because they want to train everyone to perfection as that is what they always strive for. So trying to figure out what is good enough is hard for both operations and training and is a constant challenge. Establishing the standard of 'good enough' must be considered and determined to help both smooth out training and set realistic goals during DDMA type operations.

And finally I was continually amazed by our operator's ability to deal with the daily impossible problems I mentioned earlier. Every single day they were able to come up with excellent solutions to problems. So attribute-wise, the kind of operators you need that are good at DDMA, I would say the first attribute is intelligence and the second is situational awareness. And by situational awareness I don't mean the ability to recognize a threat and engage, while understanding where your friends are and communicating with them, although that is important too. I mean a larger situational awareness where you understand the mission, cultural sensitivities, the reasons behind higher decisions and the implications of your decisions across several levels.

Indeed, this chapter has so far highlighted the need to understand the people you are working with and helping to train. Equally important, is the ability to understand the people you work for and to link the strategic to the tactical and *vice versa*.

STRATEGIC TO TACTICAL LINKAGE

Asking the operators about strategies and policies is one way to determine whether strategies and policies are recognized and implemented. According to the United States National Security Strategy one of the United States' enduring interests is the "security of the United States, its citizens, and U.S. allies and partners." One of the ways of meeting that enduring interest, in particular as it related to Iraq, is in committing to "train, equip, and advise Iraqi Security Forces" and transition security to full Iraqi responsibility.[12] In 2005 President Bush characterized the strategy. He proclaimed, "As the Iraqis stand up, we will stand down."[13]

From an operator's point of view, Master Chief Ivie comments on the progress in his small part of the training and transition effort as he prepared to depart Iraq:

> The Iraqis [Special Operations Forces], from a tactical perspective on the ground – if you were to follow them into a target, into a house or a structure, on night vision goggles; if there was a door a couple of doors down the hallway that needed to be breached, the word "breacher" would be called up and that person would run up to that door and breach that door any way he knew how, whether it was explosively or mechanically. When all the lights came on after the operation, we would find that was an Iraqi. You couldn't tell us apart – an American from an Iraqi. That's how far tactically those guys have come. After eight and a half years of training, in combat, that is where they are tactically.

Notably, he was not so optimistic that these tactical achievements will translate to strategic objectives. Ivie noted, "They [Iraqis SOF] are a very formidable force in a country which has its [own] cultural norms; it's going to take it a while to get any further; to get them above the operational level." He cautioned, "We do have some fears with the unit that it might be abused, its capabilities misused. ...[they] might be used politically as a weapon because they are so well trained. That's my biggest fear."

In a general sense, that same strategy is being used in Afghanistan. Sergeant Twomey, understanding the strategy and operating the tactical level, suggested, however that it was only to some degree being implemented:

[In 2008] The emphasis was to train our way out of a job by training and equipping the Afghan National Security Forces to stand on their own against the Taliban. Operations were "an Afghan face," partnered with ANSF as much as possible....The need to enable and empower ANSF to fight and win was clear. When I returned in 2010, the emphasis was even greater as missions without a significant and sizeable ANSF component were being rejected.

However, while tactical actions stressed developing the Afghan security capability, there seemed to be a disconnect with the overall ANSF structure design. It was not necessarily a fault with the strategy, but more so the plan and its implementation. Twomey explained, "In many ways we had a strategy to fight the war, but not necessarily to win it. The SOTF [Special Operations Task Force] had made arrangements to acquire a platoon of ANA on loan from the local brigade, and in the 15 months the task force had trained them to an outstanding standard, certainly better than the commandos or ANA SF [Special Forces] any of us had worked with." In the end however, Twomey continued, "the TOOFAN [Storm in Pashto and Dari] were never going to amount to anything, as there was no program for them to fit into. Early in our rotation when their parent brigade was transferred to Jalalabad and the TOOFAN went with them, where they were broken up as a unit and distributed to other units." He finished, "Many of them have since been killed."

US Sergeant Major Krueger had had similar experiences, in particular during the early periods of the war. In 2003, he had conducted many of their missions with the hired Afghan Security Guards (ASG). However, the ASG were not part of ANSF structure. In 2005 the leadership in-country said, according to Krueger, "Hey, no more running around with these ASG guys, the hired security guards. You have to legitimize an Afghanistan National Army or Afghan National Police force." While Sergeant Major Krueger and his team considered the direct action mission to be the easier "low hanging fruit," they subsequently recognized that FID was their primary mission. Notably, US General Stanley A. McChrystal later asked of similar teams, "Yeah, but what are you doing to work yourself out of a job?"

These examples reflect the reality of the short horizon perspective at the tactical level with tactical units rotating in every seven to twelve months. In reality the tactical operators cannot work themselves out of a job, but they can make it better for the next Coalition unit to build upon. In that way the commanders at the operational and strategic levels, with their eyes on the long horizon, are the glue that ensures the continuity at the tactical level.

TACTICAL TO STRATEGIC LINKAGE

The second part of the challenge in both Iraq and Afghanistan was linking the people to a national government they would recognize and accept as legitimate.[14] One of the programs designed to do that was Village Stability Operations. VSO are SOF supported, bottom-up stability efforts along the lines of security, governance and development designed to undermine insurgent influence and control. According to US Colonels Ty Connett and Bob Cassidy, "VSO enable local security and re-establish or re-empower traditional local governance mechanisms that represent the populations, such as shuras and jirgas (decision-making councils), and that promote critical local development to improve the quality of life within village communities and districts."[15] The intent is to connect "village clusters upward to local district centers, while national-level governance efforts connect downward to provincial centers and then to district-level centers."[16]

Sergeant Major Krueger worked the program during 2010 and cited an example of some of the challenges recognized and solved through VSO:

> These guys [SOF] were working in a village that was about 13 kilometers from the Korengal district center. 13 kilometers and one river was enough to get disconnected from the district center. And let's not forget the tribal divides that exist. There was a long standing dispute that kept two or three of the tribes from talking to each other. We finally got those guys [tribal representative] in there to sit down and talk about it. The dispute had been going on for 30 years and they were able to figure it out in less than a week just by getting them to sit down and talk.

As Krueger talked of the three basic ingredients of VSO – security, governance and development – he commented on the latter.

> Now do we [US SOF] want to be in the development work for the country? Never! But we need to bring in some quick hit projects in order to bring stability to that area to where the NGOs [Non-Governmental Organizations], or the State Department personnel, or the Afghan ministries such as the Ministry of Rural Rehabilitation and Development can come in and work.

Sergeant Major Krueger also spoke of the challenges in developing the ALP program as an integral part of the security effort. Despite the Coalition's dependence on warlords and local militia to overthrow the Taliban regime in 2001, they were an anathema to linking local security and governance to the national system.[17] Afghans, in particular those holding governmental office, associated local police with militias. As such, they had to mentally break that association between local police and militia/warlord before they could establish a local police force that would be supported by the

Afghan government. Krueger explained the negative connotations associated with the term "militia":

> So why is "militia" viewed as such a bad thing in Afghanistan? It's because in Afghanistan, people associate Militias with warlords....You've got to be careful with the ALP, that one could go south [deteriorate] in a hurry and return to warlordism. If you didn't create the connection between the local Mullahs, the elders in that community, and the district and provincial governor, then you didn't start ALP. That's one thing that the general purpose forces didn't understand – you have to have a mentorship out there to maintain a link. It wasn't that you were only going to be there for a day or two out of the week; it has to be a consistent mentorship program.

In 2010, Sergeant Twomey, while in Khakrez, was on exchange with the Village Stability Program and US Special Forces Operational Detachment 3131 and also recognized the need for a strong mentorship program. He described the situation:

> The team was located in a former school placed in the centre of approximately six villages, with another larger village also within their AO, but not within foot patrol distance. The situation on the ground was such that the small villages surrounding the VSO embed site were on one side, but not really united. The larger village was well connected and secured as the Khakrez sub-district governor was from there, and consequently there were ANP and government programs there.

Initially, Twomey looked for a way to unite the smaller villages. Since access to water seemed to be a common problem in the area, as it seemed to be throughout most of Afghanistan, he proposed the development of a water council. As he noted, "What I recommended was the establishment of a water council made up, not of village maliks (chiefs), but appointees that would speak on their behalf. Only projects approved by this council would be funded, forcing the villages to compromise and work together in setting priorities. The larger purpose of this council wasn't so much water per se, but to establish the thin edge of the wedge of governance." He continued, "If well managed and mentored, this body could be the seed that grows to take over larger responsibilities."

CONCLUSION

Each operator offered unique experiences, reinforcing the idea that "if you've seen *one* Village Stability Operation, you've seen one Village Stability Operation." Although their experiences were unique, many of those experiences and lessons emanated from the realization that operational culture, those aspects of culture that influence the outcome of a military operation, was critical to mission success.[18] As is evident, the operators frequently cited cultural characteristics that impacted their ability to train partnership forces. As trainers, teachers, mentors and coaches that lived with, ate with and fought with their partnership forces, it was all about the operators changing partner force behaviours, an incredibly difficult task, particularly in a foreign culture.

Another common theme included the challenges of linking strategic objectives to tactical actions and *vice versa*. Operators needed to know why they were in theatre and equally the local population needed to buy into this end goal for there to be a plausible exit strategy and sustainable local government.

In sum, it is unquestionable that US and Canadian SOF have entered a unique, fast-paced, complex world characterized by diverse, less recognizable threats and different and sometimes conflicting cultures. Nonetheless, there are commonalities that link operations prior to 9/11, as well as different post 9/11 theatres, at the operator level. Perhaps the Canadian Special Operations Forces Command motto, *Viam Inveniemus* (we will find a way), best reflects that commonality as the operators adapt and deal with each challenge in their own way.

NOTES

1   T.E. Lawrence, "27 Articles," *Arab Bulletin*, 20 August 1917.

2   Remarks as delivered by Secretary of Defense Robert M. Gates, at Kansas State University, Manhattan, Kansas, Monday, November 26, 2007.

3   *Sustaining Global Leadership: Priorities for the 21st Century Defense*, January 2012, 3.

4   The panel session was intended to draw on, and connect to, comments and perspectives from previous speakers and panel members. While most of the speakers spoke at the strategic and operational level, the operators provided the tactical perspective, where those policies and strategies are implemented, on the ground – where tactical applications can have operational and strategic implications.

5   Dean Robert F. Bruner, "The Role of the Student in the Case Method Classroom," Darden School of Business, University of Virginia, <http://faculty.darden.virginia.edu/brunerb/case-student.htm>, accessed on 4 March 2012.

6   This may seem incidental to some readers, but in the training and education community there are unending discussions over training versus teaching, training versus education and what is described as *how to do versus how to think*. For additional information see Knarr, Jones, L'Etoile and Hammes, *Applying Current Wars Lessons to Training and Education*, Institute for Defense Analyses Paper P-4551, December 2009.

7   William D. Wunderle continues with, "Culture is shaped by many factors, including history, religion, ethnic identity, language, and nationality," William D. Wunderle, *Through the Lens of Cultural Awareness: A Primer for US Armed Forces Deploying to Arab and Middle Eastern Countries* (Ft Leavenworth, KS: Combat Studies Inst. Press, 2006), 9.

8   LTC Scott Mann, USA, "Village Stability Engagement Plan Methodology for RC South," undated.

9   Commander's Initiative Group, Combined Forces Special Operations Component Command-Afghanistan, "Best Practices in Village Stability Operations," undated.

10   Commander's Initiative Group, Combined Forces Special Operations Component Command-Afghanistan, "Best Practices in Village Stability Operations," undated.

11   Very little editing was done by the author throughout the chapter. This section, almost in its entirety, was written by Major Suffoletta.

12   United States National Security Strategy, May 2010, p.24.

13   John D. Banusiewicz, "As the Iraqis Stand Up, We Will Stand Down," *American Forces Press Service*, 28 June 2005.

14   United States Army Field Manual 3-24, *Counterinsurgency*, December 2006.

15   Colonel Ty Connett and Colonel Bob Cassidy, USA, "Village Stability Operations: More Than a Village Defense," *Special Warfare*, July – September 2011 Edition.

16   Ibid.

17   As one example, recall the Coalition's reliance on General Rashid Dostum and his militia in Northern Afghanistan as SFODA linked up with him in October 2001. Within three weeks Mazar-e Sharif fell and was heralded as the Coalition's "First Victory of the 21st Century." Within several weeks Bagram fell and then Kabul. William Knarr and Robert Richbourg, *Learning from the First Victory of the 21st Century: Mazar-s Sharif (Revised), An Education/Training Resource*, Institute for Defense Analyses, January 2010.

18   Barak A. Salmoni and Paula Holmes-Eber, Paula, Operational Culture for the Warfighter, Principles and Applications, Marine Corps University, 2008, 15, defines operational culture as: "Those aspects of culture that influence the outcome of a military operation...."

CHAPTER 7

SOF TRAINING OTHERS:
A JOURNALIST'S PERSPECTIVE

DAVID PUGLIESE

This chapter concerns itself with a journalist's perspective on SOF training others. Notably, I have reported on conventional military training in a number of different locations from the Philippines, to Haiti, to Afghanistan. This chapter, however, will focus on Exercise Flintlock, a special operations forces training event that took place in Senegal in February and March 2011. While it is undeniable that SOF help to shape the contemporary operating environment, from a journalist's perspective their contributions are sometimes frustrating to report for supposed operational security reasons that often fluctuate between countries and even within a nation and thus appear *ad hoc* and poorly supported.

In many ways, the conventional training that I saw in locations such as the Philippines and Afghanistan was similar to what was being taught in Senegal, in the sense that many of the skills were focused on basic military instruction such as movement and navigation, patrolling and ambush tactics. Each mission, however, always maintains some degree of uniqueness.

Flintlock 11 was sponsored by US Africa Command and conducted by SOC Africa. In total, about 800 personnel were involved in Flintlock, with special operations forces operators coming from the US, Canada, Spain, France, The Netherlands and Germany. Additionally, African SOF units and personnel came from Burkina Faso, Chad, Mali, Mauritania, Nigeria and Senegal. The tactical portion of the exercise took place in Thies, Senegal while a conference bringing together western and African officers, security specialists, and academics from the region was conducted in the capital city of Dakar.

Those being trained were African SOF, although I would say the term was applied very loosely as the skill level among such troops varied extensively. In Africa, there is a tendency for parachute-qualified units and paramilitary police forces to be classified as "special."

Flintlock 11, like all such training, raised potential major issues. In order to minimize the chances of their occurrence, US military officers stated that only specific African SOF units were allowed to take part in the exercise and had to have been pre-screened in regard to human rights issues by the US State Department. In addition, another criteria was that the units being trained had to be involved in countering drug or weapons smuggling, or directly involved in fighting terrorist organizations such as Al-Qaeda in the Islamic Maghreb or AQIM.

The idea behind these stipulations was that it would supposedly help rule out units who could use their training against the general population in their countries. However, there was an acknowledgement among US officers that there are no, and could never be any, guarantees that such a situation would never occur.

In fact, there are already examples of such abuses. In 2011, the *Globe and Mail* newspaper carried a report that linked police in South Sudan, who had been trained by the Royal Canadian Mounted Police (RCMP) and Canadian provincial police forces, to a vicious crackdown to enforce conservative dress among women and young men. Police abused women who dared to wear trousers and men who had grown dreadlocks were beaten and then had their hair cut forcibly by police.

Indeed, the issue of human rights abuses is a minefield that each training mission will have to confront, with no guarantees that the skills special operations forces impart will not be used later to suppress local populations. While a few paragraphs cannot due the topic justice, for the purpose of this chapter it suffices to highlight the issue.

From a media perspective, the coverage of Flintlock was a cross-section of interests that reflected each news outlet's particular coverage focus. My assignment was to concentrate on the activities of the CSOR since the newspaper I work for – the *Ottawa Citizen* – considers the regiment, with a home base of Canadian Forces Base Petawawa in the Ottawa Valley, to be a local unit.

For the *Ottawa Citizen*, the aim was to tie in an international training event with a local unit. Notably, a sidebar article was also done on the issue of human rights concerns and such training. Moreover, I wrote other articles on the threat posed by AQIM in the region, in addition to an article on Robert Fowler, the Ottawa-based diplomat who had been kidnapped several years ago by AQIM. (Again, you can see that local focus in our coverage.)

From a broader perspective, CNN focused on US special operations forces as well as CSOR, tying their coverage into the AQIM issue. Senegalese media reported on the foreign military involvement in Flintlock and the fact that Senegalese forces were coordinating much of the exercise.[1] A secondary theme in such coverage was the ongoing issue for many nations in the region about whether Africa Command (AFRICOM) will establish a permanent headquarters in Africa.

In my experience, CSOR was open and accommodating. The Canadian Special Operations Forces Command's public affairs team had laid much of the groundwork in advance so the unit members understood what I was interested in and ensured that I saw anything I wanted to see.

Additionally, US Army Green Beret Lieutenant-Colonel Chris Schmitt, one of the Flintlock planners, answered any question put to him with an openness and bluntness that I found extremely refreshing, particularly considering the current situation Canadian journalists face with the Department of National Defence and the conventional side of the Canadian Forces which answer most media queries via emailed "talking points."

That is not to say that there were no problems, however. The Department of Foreign Affairs and International Trade had a representative at the main base in Thies but he/she would carefully move around location to avoid me as they did not want the Department's interest in the training exercise reported. Notably, this desire for anonymity existed despite the fact I had already reported that DFAIT was involved in the Canadian portion of Flintlock. In fact, I was told at one point that this individual was worried I would find out that an African soldier had been killed in a road accident while off duty during Flintlock. My response to the military officer informing me about this concern was that I had not traveled 6,000 kilometers to report on a road fatality in a country where driving habits appeared to be learned from the movie "Death Race".

French media had a different take on the situation. A TV crew had travelled from Paris at great expense and felt frustrated by their Flintlock experience. I could understand this sentiment. Unlike print journalism, TV requires much more visuals as well as on-camera interviews. They had expected more openness and complained they spent much of their time sitting around the public affairs office at the main base. They had thought they could interview African officers and soldiers but this was not possible because those nations strictly controlled media access in that regard. They had also thought they could interview French SOF who were participating in Flintlock but this was not possible as the French wanted to keep a low profile. The news crew interpreted these decisions as an attempt to hide some nefarious motives and at least one of their journalists came to see Flintlock as being more than just a training mission to help Africans and instead an exercise to aid the US in establishing more of a foothold on the African continent in order to exploit oil and other natural resources.

This journalist's concerns about excessive secrecy were not alleviated when she was told she could get all the interviews she desired with African officials and an overall greater picture of the war against AQIM if she travelled to Dakar where the main conference was being held. She was told that a Canadian Forces CANSOFCOM major could help her. The major, of course – who had no idea this was happening – would not have been able to speak on these issues as his area of expertise was CSOR's involvement in Flintlock and nothing more. He had nothing to do with this situation, and unknown to him, he was being used a decoy – if you will – to get rid of the journalist. Needless to say, this action probably did not help Flintlock coverage in France.

Obviously, to an outsider, the issue of operational security was interesting, to say the least. CSOR has gone through a number of variations regarding operational security. When I first covered the unit's initial selection process in Kamloops, British Columbia in 2006, the regiment made the decision to allow operators to be identified by only their first names. For Flintlock, this process was still the case, although I understand now that there has been a decision to allow the use of full names if an operator so desires.

Journalists covering Flintlock were told under no circumstances could they take photographs of operators from any country taking part in the exercise, unless it was a photograph taken from a very long distance away or from behind or from the side of that individual. In terms of OPSEC, this direction went awry. CSOR operators did not have any issues with photographs being taken, as long as they had sunglasses or hats on that helped obscure their identities. They used their first names, ages, ranks and hometowns.

US Navy SEALs at Flintlock had a strict OPSEC policy and that was rigidly followed. When I interviewed two SEALs at Flintlock for *Seapower Magazine*, an American-based publication, I was told no photographs at all were allowed. Additionally, there would be no first names, no last names, no ages, no hometowns, and no reference to previous deployments that these individual SEALs had undertaken (i.e., to Afghanistan or Iraq). Notably, I find it quite interesting that actual SEALs are now featured in a new Hollywood movie as well as on the cover of a romance novel just published in the US. But times change, I guess.

Those from the US Marine Corps Special Operations Command (MARSOC) were not too concerned about photographs, and decided to allow last names – not first names – to be used by journalists. Spanish SOF did TV interviews using their full names and with their faces exposed. In the case of US Army Green Berets who were working with CSOR training Malian soldiers, I was originally told operational security rules dictated they could not appear in any photographs and it was best that I stay out of their way. But within twenty minutes of my arrival at the training camp, the two Green Berets came and introduced themselves. When I mentioned that I would try to keep them out of my photographs for the stated security reasons, they responded that they had no concerns at all and to photograph as much as I wanted.

As such, my concluding message is to have a consistent operational security policy when it comes to such training missions. I lost track of all the different guidelines I had been given during Flintlock when it came to OPSEC. But instead of going to the natural default position of being as secretive as possible, my recommendation would be to lean towards as much openness as possible. That would allow potential misunderstandings about Defence, Diplomacy and Military Assistance missions to be addressed and dealt with.

NOTES

1   As an aside, journalists informed me that it is a common fixture at media events in Senegal for government and other agencies to provide a local reporter with an envelope of money at the beginning of the press conference. This practice is to offset their meager wages, and some would argue to buy positive coverage.

CHAPTER 8

WORKING WITH OTHERS: SIMPLE GUIDELINES TO MAXIMIZE EFFECTIVENESS

DR. EMILY SPENCER AND COLONEL BERND HORN, Phd

Teamwork is often a sacrosanct principle for achieving difficult tasks and is based on the belief that the collective effort of the whole is often stronger than any single individual could achieve working alone. In the military, especially in special operations forces, working in small teams is critical to mission success. Nonetheless, working with others is rarely easy. Different personalities, individual circumstances and the situation, as well as differing interpretations and expectations, complicate interpersonal relations and make working in teams a challenging process. These challenges are exacerbated when dealing with individuals from other nations, whether allies, coalition partners or other countries. Under these circumstances, different languages and cultures may increase the level of complexity and difficulty involved in working effectively with others.

Given the challenges of group work it is important to remain focused on the mission at hand. In fact, in order to maximize productivity and minimize tensions, there are a number of principles that can assist with providing the proper mindset when working with others. As such, this chapter is designed to help individuals conducting training missions or operations, particularly with other organizations or armed forces. These principles have been derived from personal experience, as well as numerous interviews with those who have worked extensively with others in training, mentoring and/or operational roles. Importantly, these principles also provide a good guideline for any type of group endeavour.

PART I – BUILDING EFFECTIVE RELATIONSHIPS

In brief, the ten "simple" principles of working effectively with others are as follows:

1. Be patient;

2. Be adaptable and manage your expectations;

3. Recognize that actions speak louder than words;

4. Appreciate that perception is more important than reality;

5. Remember that the message sent is not always the message that is received and it is the message that is received that is acted on;

6. See the world through the eyes of those with whom you are interacting;

7. Do not judge the behaviours of others and, instead, observe, learn and try to understand;

8. Always be respectful;

9. Deal with frustrations privately; and

10. Do not adhere to unrealistic standards.

Although these principles may seem simplistic and elicit the criticism that they are "motherhood statements," their application is often difficult and many individuals fail miserably in putting them into practice, particularly in a training environment. As such, it is well worthwhile to give thought to what they actually mean in order to appreciate how they can contribute to effective relationship building. After all, being aware of a potential problem is the first step to solving it.

1. Be patient.

On the whole, Western society has seemingly become a whirlwind of activity and expectations. Fuelled by a myriad of social networking devices, widespread communication networks and infrastructures, technological innovation and accessibility, and increasingly user-friendly and accessible services (e.g. mail-ordered products, drive-through banking, coffee, meals, even weddings, etc.), people have become more and more impatient and expectant of instant gratification and results with little to no human interaction required. For the most part, people are no longer willing to wait for what they want.

Western military members are not immune to the world of instant gratification that engulfs many industrialized nations. Indeed, the aggressive, hyper, military work ethic and results-orientated attitude of SOF operators can simply add fuel to the fire when requirements are not being met. These characteristics, which are generally seen as desirable among SOF operators, can nonetheless contribute to misunderstandings, frustrations and even personal conflict when interacting with other people's expectations and beliefs about how the world works, or at least should work.

When working with others it is important to realize that your schedule is not always a valid blueprint for success. Not all countries, cultures and people are accustomed to, or accepting of, the Western industrialized tempo of activity, much less that of a SOF level of activity. Impatience and trying to force others to work at your accepted rhythm can be counterproductive and create alienation and bad feelings.

As such, it is always important to try and determine the geographic and cultural dynamics of why there are delays to achieving the expected results. Always remember that there could be a number of reasons for the slower than desired execution of activities on the part of others. Part of the problem could be a question of re-sourcing. Often things such as transport, logistical support and even photocopying etc., items Canadian SOF may take for granted, are not readily available. Nonetheless, these delays may be the norm for the group of people working within these circumstances and can lead to the expectation of a slow tempo. Additionally, one needs to consider that training partners may not want to share these realities with you due to potential embarrassment over their lack of resources. In addition, geographic and subsequent cultural dynamics may also be at play. For example, people living in southern regions that suffer from excessive heat have adjusted their pace of life accordingly over time. The culture most likely has adopted an attitude to dealing with the sustained long-term condition. Parachuting in for a short duration and expecting all to adapt to the faster tempo may be an imposition that is not welcomed or accepted.

As such, patience is an important quality to minimize stress and maintain personal equilibrium. It is also important in maintaining good relations with those with whom you are working. Additionally, it demonstrates professionalism and an ability to adapt and innovate.

In the end, when working with others, it is important to be mentally prepared to adapt to the unique set of circumstances that is present. Steel your mind with the understanding that patience and self-discipline will always be necessary and contribute more to mission success than a frenzied approach that will likely do more to aggravate the situation than contribute to a solution.

2. Be adaptable and manage your expectations.

Theory and practice are often worlds apart. Indeed, the best plans and ambitions may not survive contact with the training audience. It is important to plan to a high standard and set ambitious goals but, above all, they must be achievable. Important in this respect is to set and promulgate clear and realistic objectives. Nonetheless, ensure that you prepare yourself to adjust according to circumstances on the ground, whether due to weather, terrain, personnel or equipment. Understand that various dynamics that you do not control will undoubtedly change the schedule, your plan and potentially even your training objectives.

The key to adapting and providing valuable training is the realization that you are there to work with the partner nation or training audience and, more often than not, they will determine the schedule. The fact of the matter is that not all countries have the same resources as North American SOF. Moreover, their organizational culture will often be dramatically different. As a result, try to learn as much about the training audience as possible. Develop a plan you feel meets the aim of the mission. Do your best to execute according to the plan but realize you may have to adjust the schedule, plan, level of instruction and/or outcomes. Do not let this frustrate you but rather remain open-minded and agile in your thinking so that you can rise to the challenge and create the necessary effect. Additionally, remember it is better to under-program and be able to add extra activities that were not scheduled than it is to over-program and not achieve the promulgated training. The first carries a nuance of excelling and achieving more than anticipated while the latter carries an undercurrent of failure.

3. Recognize that actions speak louder than words.

As the adage goes, talk is cheap. It is easy to create a verbal image of yourself or your organization in an attempt to create credibility. However, if you are unknown to a training audience, this verbiage will likely be inconsequential. You must remember that actions speak louder than words. Never explain what you can demonstrate. Credibility and trust are based on actions, not just words. The sooner you can show the training audience that you are an expert at what you do, the sooner they will give you their undivided attention.

Conversely, it is important to also consider the reverse. The description of capability that your training audience may have expressed is not always an accurate reflection of their ability. Before undertaking complex, potentially hazardous, activities, ensure you determine the level of competency and capacity of your partners through actions not just words. This knowledge will help you determine the level of training, rehearsals, planning, etc. that will be necessary prior to the event. It may entail lowering or raising the level of activity previously envisioned but either way it will maximize time and effort and lead to a greater overall effect. Importantly, exercise tact when "organizing" an opportunity to observe capability.

4. **Appreciate that perception is more important than reality.**

Quite often we discount the opinions, criticism, or comments of others because, rightly or wrongly, we feel they are not accurate reflections of the reality on the ground. The attitude of "well that's what they may think but the truth is completely different," often staves away acting on perceived problems or grievances. However, perception often becomes reality. How the training audience or partners perceive you or the mission is more important than the reality you are convinced exists. For example, your mission might be critical to providing them with important training, and you and your team may be the eminent experts in the field and the best and most personable operators on the globe. Nonetheless, if those you are trying to help feel the activity is a waste of their time and you as the trainers are a bunch of arrogant, pompous, over-rated or second-rate players, the task will become difficult, if not impossible, to accomplish. In this case, the perception is more important than the reality.

When trying to get buy-in from others, what is important is not what you think but rather what they think. Therefore, ensure you keep abreast of atmospherics and the general prevailing attitude and work quickly and aggressively to clear-up any misunderstandings, grievances or complaints.

In the end, communications are key to developing any partnership. It is critical to always attempt to provide others with a clear understanding of the five "Ws" (what, where, why, who and when), as well as "how", to avoid confusion and misunderstanding. Finally, explain any changes to the plan and immediately address any misperceptions that may have been, or are, developing. Never assume your impression of yourself or of the activity you are undertaking is the same as everyone else's and continuously do your best to mitigate any potential differences.

5. **Remember that the message sent is not always the message that is received and it is the message that is received that is acted on.**

Communications are often "lost in translation." Simply put, the message you think you are sending is not always the message that the intended recipient is actually understanding and acting on. There are a number of reasons for this disconnect. First, we often use words, jargon, slang and concepts that we are familiar with but that have different meanings to different people, particularly when they are from different cultures. Even within the same language set, the meaning is not always the same.

In addition, we are all often guilty of a lack of clarity in our communications. In our minds we understand the situation, and what we are thinking and communicating is crystal clear to us. However, what we forget is that in communicating we often leave out key information that is assumed as "understood" between the parties. As a result, for those not privy to the inner workings of another's mind it becomes difficult to follow and the message or intent is confusing. As such, ensure you properly formulate your message. Do not assume the receiver is privy to all you know or are thinking.

Due to these factors, it is important to actively confirm and ensure that the message you are sending is actually the message that is being received and that it is not being "lost in translation." To do so you can, among other things, ask the person you are dealing with to explain the concept/idea back to you in his or her words; observe the individual explaining the concept/idea to a larger group; or ask for the best method to carry out the task and determine if it makes sense.

Communications are key to the success of virtually any activity, particularly when working with others. They are not something that should be taken for granted or assumed. A major effort must go into communications, whether non-verbal, verbal or written, to ensure the intent, spirit and exact meaning of the written or spoken word are accurately delivered and received.

6. See the world through the eyes of those with whom you are interacting.

Culture and experience are powerful forces. Our attitudes, and consequently behaviours, are shaped by our beliefs and values which in turn are formulated through cultural understandings and personal experiences. These lenses create a filter through which we see the world, which in turn shapes how we react to stimuli.

Notably, assumptions, priorities and even our definition of "ground truth" will often vary significantly from those with whom you are working. Therefore, it is vital to be able to see the world through the eyes of those with whom you are interacting if you wish to have a desired impact. Our assumptions of the world and how things are done are not universal. How we do things will not always be how others will conduct drills and/or training activities nor will it be necessarily representative of how they want to conduct their business. Furthermore, as mentioned, what we take for granted (e.g. availability of transport, logistical and administrative support, training area, etc.) may be a major challenge for others. Thus, to achieve a desired effect, it is important to see their perception of reality.

Additionally, this perspective will help you appreciate how others see you. Your mannerisms, assumptions, attitudes and behaviours may not be acceptable to those you are working with. For example, although Canadian Special Operations Forces personnel pride themselves on being "straight shooters"/"speaking truth to power"/being able to critically assess and challenge one another in an open setting, these types of behaviours are often seen as aggressive and offensive to others given their organizational culture. Understanding how others see the world may help you realize that the way you see yourself is actually quite different than the way they do.

As such, you should learn how to read the body language of others in order to gain cues about how your behaviour is being interpreted. Additionally, learn to self-reflect and assess your personality and personal approach prior to working with others. However, if your self-assessment fails you, be prepared to adapt your behaviour/deportment accordingly based on the reactions from those around you. If you feel you must apologize for your behaviour prior to even beginning your statement, such as beginning a talk with the words "I don't mean to be rude, but ..." you should likely stop immediately and reassess the situation. If you identify that what you are about to say is potentially offensive, then it probably is and you should find a different way of expressing your point.

In the end, if developing a partnership or simply working with others is important to your task, then it is critical that you take the time to reflect on, assess, and understand "reality" as it is seen by those you work with. You need not philosophically accept their outlook or version of reality, but you need to understand it and how it will affect their attitudes and behaviours, as well as how it impacts on your attitudes and behaviours.

7. Do not judge the behaviours of others and, instead, observe, learn and try to understand.

It is always important not to exude an attitude of arrogance and/ or superiority. Quite often, many of the personnel who are part of the training audience have a depth of operational experience in their own country or from other missions. They all have unique operating circumstances, cultural dynamics, and traditions, habits and attitudes. Simply because it is not "how we do things" does not mean it is wrong, invalid or inappropriate to the specific situation or socio-cultural-geographic area. As such, it is best never to simply judge a behaviour without fully understanding it. Rather, observe and learn what you can that may assist your own skills and comprehension of working in the geographic area.[1] Provide commentary on how you and your organization would handle a similar situation but do so in an anecdotal and descriptive manner that explains your methodology and philosophical approach rather than providing a judgemental comparison or critique.

In the end, do not try to tell others what to do and/or how to do it. You do not live in their reality. Something may work well for you and your organization but it may not fit in their context/reality.

However, do not give anyone the benefit of the doubt. Check and confirm that they have the requisite skill/knowledge/background/ qualifications required before undertaking an activity, particularly if it is a hazardous one.

8. Always be respectful.

Everyone is more cooperative when treated respectfully. Nonetheless, quite often we fail to demonstrate respect. In fact, on many occasions individuals, without even consciously knowing it, will act disrespectfully or at least be perceived to be doing so. Particularly when in a training or mentor role in a foreign cultural setting, one's behaviour might be seen as being dismissive, overly casual with those of senior rank and, at times, even rude, especially when things are not going as planned or according to the "time table" and patience is wearing thin. Additionally, what one might consider a show of confidence might instead be interpreted as arrogance, with obvious negative effect. Finally, though humility is touted as a SOF virtue, equally, if not more often, hubris and ego show through and some individuals feel their status as a specialist or expert merits special status compared to others, an anathema to equality and respect.

How you treat and interact with others is important. Treating others with respect conveys a valuable message of not only what you, but also your organization deem is important. It demonstrates character, humility and professionalism. Within the military, nowhere is this more evident than in according the proper deference and respect to military protocol when dealing with those of higher rank, a fact that is sometimes neglected by some SOF personnel. This behaviour underscores respect of the individual and their national armed forces and speaks to professionalism and humility.

Additionally, it is important to understand that as the trainer, mentor, or partner you represent your organization and your nation. Your behaviour will not only determine how others see you, but also how they will form their perceptions of all other national representatives, both SOF and conventional forces.

As such, being respectful of others is an important enabler. It can generate goodwill, cooperation and friendship; lack of respect will deteriorate these factors. Additionally, respect demonstrates professionalism and helps to foster the bonds that create personal and organizational networks. Respect is a key ingredient in establishing and maintaining positive relationships.

9. Deal with frustrations privately.

It is always important to be conscious of how others see you. At times, your true feelings may be counterproductive to the task at hand. On these occasions, it is best to remain focused on your goal and to refrain from showing counterproductive thoughts and/or emotions. This advice is particularly valid when frustrated. At such points you must be particularly conscious of your body language (e.g. rolling of the eyes, posture, muttering, impatience, etc). Although easier said than done, remain calm and unperturbed at all times as showing frustration will only erode trust and credibility and make the task more difficult. Deal with frustration once in the privacy of your living quarters. Rant and complain to your close colleagues. Discuss the frustration and pet peeves with the team in private when those you are training are not around. Always ensure you are in a secure location where you cannot be overheard by others. However, in the presence of others calm, cool, patient behaviour will earn trust and respect and will strengthen personal relationships. Failure to do so will have exactly the opposite effect.

10. Do not adhere to unrealistic standards.

Striving for excellence is a noble pursuit and one should never adopt an attitude of accepting mediocrity. However, one must be conscious of time and resource realities and how much one can realistically achieve under these circumstances. As such, incremental steps to improve should be accepted and applauded. Excellence can only be achieved once the foundation is solid. Building a foundation takes time and experience, which may not be immediately available. Learning incrementally in these instances may be the best course of action.

In this vein, it is better that the training audience accomplish a task themselves, even if it is "a bit rougher around the edges" than if you had conducted the major actions for them. Remember you are there to help train and mentor, not to overtake their areas of responsibility. View excellence as a long-term goal and always strive towards it, but do so along a graduated scale so that the training audience develops the necessary skills and attributes, as well as confidence. This process will help build a solid foundation upon which to improve and attain professional excellence.

PART II – DEBRIEFING OTHERS

Part of working with others, particularly in a training role, is assessing strengths and weakness, what went right and what went wrong, and, of course, how to improve performance, as well as tactics, techniques and procedures. The process of constructively providing feedback on ways to improve is never easy, however. It is always a fine line, often due to personal perceptions about what is deemed personal criticism and what is professional observation/constructive criticism. As such, there are also a number of "considerations" that should be kept in mind when providing feedback. These include:

1. Being respectful, particularly when speaking to someone of higher rank;

2. Never being condescending;

3. Remembering that a few key points are more manageable than providing an overwhelming number of areas to improve on;

4. Being conscious of the words you choose;

5. Attempting to have individuals identify their weaknesses/ failures/areas to improve themselves;

6. Utilizing techniques that make use of sound operational experience;

7. Using non-attribution when providing constructive criticism;

8. Ensuring you always include at least some positive feedback;

9. Rewarding the behaviour/activity you are trying to promote; and

10. Remembering not to take anything personally.

1. Be respectful, particularly when speaking to someone of higher rank.

As mentioned, it is important to always show respect. In particular during debriefs, ensure that cultural dynamics are considered and addressed. For instance, some militaries have a very conservative and traditional culture. For example, they may have a culture of engendering trust in the officer and/or stress the separation of rank, particularly at the officer level. As such, it is important to demonstrate that you respect their military culture and protocol, regardless of your own practices with regard to debriefing training activities. Where possible try to have officers debriefing officers, senior non-commissioned officers (NCOs) debriefing peers etc. Again, this process is meant to show respect for their system and provide the best possible advice to improve their performance without creating undue tension for the training audience.

Additionally, use discretion when debriefing others, particularly when there are negative messages to pass along. Always follow the mantra "praise in public, counsel in private."

2. Never be condescending.

Never exude an attitude of superiority or put yourself in a position where that impression might be drawn by others. Avoid standing aloof and becoming the arrogant visitors who think they are better than those they are working with. Never stand at a distance and assess; rather, mingle, eat and talk with the training audience/personnel from the partner nations. Participate in activities, (although be careful not to overshadow). Work actively to build relationships. Share experiences and approaches. Ask questions and show interest in their methodologies and experiences. Treat your training partners as equals. Rather than criticize, explain how your organization handles similar situations. Use operational experience as a means of helping them develop better TTPs. For example, share that certain equipment or techniques did not perform as well as expected on real operations and how the shortcomings were overcome. This explanation becomes an indirect means of "correcting" deficiencies without blatantly criticizing their way of doing things.

3. **Remember, a few key points are more manageable than providing an overwhelming number of areas to improve on.**

When working with others there is often a desire to do everything, fix all perceived shortcomings or deficiencies, and cram as much into a short period of time as possible. This process can lead to frustration, impatience and an end-state where not everything gets accomplished and everyone feels rushed and seemingly lacking a sense of real accomplishment. Moreover, although a wide range of skills were introduced, no-one feels expert or competent in any of them. This situation should be avoided. It is important to consider the audience, to understand their level of knowledge and experience, language of instruction, cultural predilections, expectations and requirements. This consideration will go a long way to dictating how much, and what form of training should take place.

The key is to focus on a few key training points, skills, or issues. Do not try and fix everything all at once or cover too wide a spectrum of training activities. In the same vein, keep advice or critique points to only a few key/critical issues that can be absorbed. Do not inundate others with lots of minutiae that bury the really important points to be addressed. It is better to ensure one or just a few skills, attributes, activities, etc. are mastered as opposed to introducing a wide spectrum of such matters that are subsequently lost, forgotten or poorly practiced and executed because they were not adequately learned. By ensuring a limited focus that allows the mastery of a subject matter, one builds a base that can then be expanded on. Failing to create a solid foundation condemns individuals and organizations to perpetual basic level instruction that does not allow them to evolve.

4.   Be conscious of the words you choose.

As explained earlier, just because you may be speaking the same language does not necessarily mean that words or phrases you are using have the exact same meaning to all parties. Do not assume all words/concepts have the same meaning in a different culture even though the language may be the same. This practice is particularly true when using jargon or slang specific to a country or organization. Therefore, be careful of the words you choose. Avoid confusing the audience and, as an added benefit, you will also avoid creating extra frustrations for yourself. Use only terms and concepts of which all share a common understanding. Additionally, ensure that you confirm this shared understanding. Be conscious of rank, position and/or situation. Remember not all organizational cultures are similar to your own. Many militaries, whether SOF or not, have more rigid hierarchical cultures that maintain strict barriers between the enlisted ranks, senior NCOs and officers. Moreover, many cultures place great emphasis on "saving face" and derogatory/disrespectful words (or those perceived as such) will have a very negative effect. For example, if swearing is common practice within your organization, do not assume that it is acceptable in a different environment.

5. Attempt to have individuals identify their weaknesses/failures/areas to improve themselves.

Avoid lecturing or directly criticizing others. Although we normally soften criticism with platitudes of how well an event went and what great improvement was shown, receiving negative criticism (sometimes known as constructive criticism) is always hard for people to take, particularly from others from a different organization/country, and especially from individuals who may hold a lower rank. As such, attempt to do a mutual assessment of the exercise. Rather than lecture, attempt to draw out the points from the individuals themselves. Start with asking what they felt they (or better yet, if applicable, what "we") did right. Then ask what they felt they/we could have done better or what they think they can improve on for the next time. If this draws a blank, provide observations that are based upon your own experience. For example, "one of the things I noticed that we have always had trouble with...." Individuals are always more open to critique when it is not specifically targeted at them and when it is made to appear as a point of weakness or difficulty for others practicing the same craft. Always be conscious of personal feelings and allow everyone to "save face". One need not lie or turn a blind eye, but remember it is all about communicating effectively and building personal relationships.

6. Utilize techniques that make use of sound operational experience.

Everyone values operational experience. After all, training is designed to prepare individuals for operations and combat. As realistic as we try to make training, it never fully replicates the real thing. Therefore, whenever possible, utilize real operational experience, case studies, events or TTPs to underline a training point. Utilize techniques such as "we've found by experience that ..... works even better/is more efficient. ...." This takes some the sting out of personal critique. It is no longer perceived as one individual's, or organization's, theoretical or doctrinal approach; rather it is seen as a proven operational methodology. In addition, it also underscores your organization's experience and current relevance in the field in question.

7. Always use non-attribution when providing constructive criticism.

As explained, choose only a few debrief points to pass on after any given activity. Focus on the key issues that will have the greatest impact and effect the greatest improvement. When commenting, avoid singling out negative individual behaviour in a group situation. Speak to actions in a general manner thereby focusing more on the collective rather than an individual. By utilizing "we" rather than "you" or naming individuals, there is less of a personal sting to the comments. If individuals need to be debriefed on actions, ensure they are taken aside privately, preferably by a peer or superior, and counselled accordingly. Importantly, remember that you are there to work with them, provide advice, assist them in improving specific skills, practices, and perhaps a degree of interoperability; notably, you are not there to make them a reflection of your organization.

8. Ensure you always include at least some positive feedback.

No-one likes to be dumped on or made to feel that everything they did was not up to standard. As such, always provide positive feedback. Find something to speak about that was legitimately well done, even if just speaking to motivation, energy, effort, etc. Do not forget that you must be honest and ensure your comments are genuine or else the words of praise will be seen as hollow platitudes and you will lose trust and credibility. When debriefing start and end your comments with something positive or, at a minimum, end on a high with positive commentary.

9. Reward the behaviour/activity you are trying to promote.

As noted earlier, actions speak louder than words. It is not what people say or write that is a true indicator of what is important to them; rather, it is what they do that really shows what is important to them. By rewarding or showing active encouragement/ support for the actions/behaviours you are trying to reinforce, you will reinforce what you are trying to achieve and the desired standard. Reward behaviours that you desire in a culturally correct way. To do so, you will need to know what motivates them. Learn quickly the drivers to performance, as well as what creates a lack of motivation. As a general rule, honest praise works wonders. As with everything, however, do so in moderation. Praise should be used to reward the behaviour/actions you wish to promote but, if overdone, it loses its value. In particularly special cases, the use of "coins" and/or other tokens takes the idea a further step. But again, it must be done in moderation in order to maintain the "specialness" of the gesture.

10. Remember not to take anything personally.

There are an infinite amount of challenges to working in cross-cultural groups. It is important to strive for your best while also ensuring that you do not take all setbacks personally. Many challenges will not be directly related to how you comport yourself and these obstacles, while potentially surmountable, may take years to overcome. Strive for perfection but bear in mind the difficulty of your task and that you are being seen not only as an individual but also a member of a specific group to which others have already made long-standing assumptions and judgements.

Moreover, accept that others may not wish to accept what you have to say. Remember, they have their own way of doing things and, importantly, live in a reality to which you are not totally familiar. Provide the best advice and support possible. Always, explain your rationale and the logic behind your comments. Provide them with your experience and wisdom. And then, step back and allow them to determine how best they wish to use your input.

CONCLUSION

In today's contemporary operating environment (COE) success is often dependent on winning the support of the people, whether the domestic population who ultimately drive government engagements across the globe, or the host-nation population that is instrumental in force effectiveness and operations within the theatre of operations. As such, understanding those with whom you interact is critical. In particular, understanding the beliefs, values, attitudes and behaviours of a group of people can mean the difference between success and failure.

This chapter was designed to provide some practical advice and tips on working with others, as well as debriefing others. Although outwardly simplistic and in some ways "motherhood" statements, the reality is that in practice these principles are often forgotten, ignored or simply poorly executed. What must always be remembered is that working with others entails relationships, which are always difficult. As such, communications, common sense and a concerted effort at understanding the dynamics of working in a group are critical to success. Hopefully, these pointers (and in many cases reminders) will be of assistance to those who are tasked with building partnerships at home and abroad.

ANNEX A

UNDERSTANDING CULTURE

In order to work effectively in cross-cultural settings, which is representative of many contemporary work environments, understanding culture and how it shapes personal perceptions is often paramount to achieving one's goals. Undeniably, understanding others is a critical enabler when trying to build partnerships whether at home or abroad. As such a conceptual understanding of culture becomes very important.

In the simplest of terms, culture refers to a set of common beliefs and values within a group of people that, combined, transform into attitudes that are expressed as behaviours.[2] (See Figure 1) Culture helps to create individual and group identity. Cultural beliefs, values and attitudes are generally long lasting and resistant to change. They are passed down through generations and are often unconscious in nature.

FIGURE 1. The Relationship between Beliefs, Values, Attitudes and Behaviours[3]

Beliefs

Beliefs represent perceived "facts" about the world (and beyond) that do not require evaluation or proof of their correctness. For example, Hindus believe in many gods, Christians believe in one God and Muslims believe in Allah. None of these competing religious "beliefs" has been unequivocally proven correct. Some beliefs may even continue to be held within a group of people in spite of refuting "facts." This can lead to attribution errors in which a cause and effect relationship is misconceived because of the rigidity of a certain belief. For instance, if you believed without question that

127

technology improves quality of life, then, as technology advanced, you would either take it for granted that quality of life was also on the rise, or, faced with blatant evidence to the contrary, you would assume that it was not technology that caused this decline. Despite the limitations that certain beliefs place on an individual or group's ability to fully evaluate their surroundings, common beliefs remain at the core of cultural identity.

Values

Values place a moral and/or pragmatic weight on beliefs. For instances, Christians do not simply believe in God, they use this belief to build an understanding of what is important in life. In this sense, "Christian values," provide a type of moral shorthand for determining "right" from "wrong." From a pragmatic perspective, if you believe that university education enables individuals to earn more over the course of a lifetime, and economic advancement is something that you deem important, then you will attach a high worth, or "value" to university education.

Believes + Values

The relationships between beliefs and values are complex and dynamic. Values are generally attached to beliefs, yet adhering to certain values can also strengthen beliefs or create new ones. Paradoxically, individuals and groups can simultaneously have competing beliefs and values. Often the weight attached to a certain belief will determine the course of action. For example, a moderate pacifist may at once be against all forms of violence and also believe strongly in self-preservation and the right to self-defence. In a situation in which the alternatives are shoot or be shot, this pacifist might choose to kill his/her attacker. In the same situation, someone with strong pacifist beliefs may rather be shot than go against his/her pacifist beliefs. Thus, what may appear as irrational to some may be completely sane and logical to others based on their beliefs and values.

Attitudes

In combination, beliefs and values create attitudes. Attitudes reflect a consistent emotional response to a belief-value pair. To change an attitude, either the belief or its associated value must be altered. To return to a previous example, if you believe that university education increases lifetime earnings and you value economic incentives, then you will have a positive attitude towards higher education. For your attitude toward higher education to change, either you must no longer believe that education leads to higher earnings, or the value that you place on economic incentives must be altered. Notably, many belief-value pairs may combine to form, strengthen or weaken an attitude. To continue with the university education example, in addition to higher earnings, you might also believe that a university education allows for more career flexibility, something that you consider to be important to quality of life. Your positive attitude towards higher education would thus be strengthened.

It is important to see attitudes as distinct from simply the combination of beliefs and values because once formed they may not be so easily broken down into their component parts and it is attitudes, rather than simply beliefs and values, which predict behaviours. That being said, however, the best way to alter attitudes is to target their core belief-value pairs with the understanding that there could be several pairs in operation at once. Notably, information and knowledge can help create a shift in attitudes.

Behaviours

Behaviour is the way in which individuals express themselves and, for the purposes of our discussion, can be verbal or non-verbal. In addition to being influenced by attitudes, motivation plays a role determining behaviour. Motivation can be influenced by the strength of beliefs and values that form attitudes (internal motivation) or it can be external, such bribery, yet the applicability of external influences will also be influenced by beliefs, values and attitudes. For example, bribing someone with money to motivate a certain behaviour would only work if that person valued money.

Culture

It is often helpful to conceptualize culture as an iceberg. In this way, beliefs, values and attitudes represent about ninety per cent of the cultural iceberg yet remain hidden from sight. Behaviours, representing a mere ten per cent or so of the cultural iceberg are, however, the only observable part of culture. (See Figure 2.)

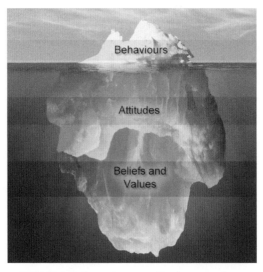

FIGURE 2. Culture Conceptualized as an Iceberg

Culture is expressed through shared behaviours that include language, religion, work habits, recreation practices, etc. It helps people to classify their experiences and communicate them symbolically. Generally, our daily lives reflect our beliefs, values and attitudes in a multitude of ways. They shape our lives and contribute to our sense of identity. Culture influences what we do and who we think we are. Additionally, our beliefs, values and attitudes, as demonstrated through our behaviours, also shape how others see us. As such, examining a region's history, their expression of self and group identity, religious practices and affiliations, their distribution of power and resources, and their mean of communication are all valuable indicators of underlying group beliefs, values and attitudes.

CULTURAL INTELLIGENCE

Cultural Intelligence (CQ) is the ability to understand the beliefs, values, attitudes and behaviours of a group of people and, most importantly, to apply this knowledge toward a specific goal. Not surprisingly, CQ is a vital component of working effectively with indigenous forces. In order to behave appropriately, CANSOF personnel need to understand the national objective or goal, have the proper region specific knowledge/awareness, and have the ability and/or skill set and motivation to exhibit appropriate behaviour. (See Figure 3.)

Clear national objective or goal

Region specific knowledge/ awareness

Mission Success

Ability and/or skill set and motivation

Appropriate Behaviour

FIGURE 3. CQ Components

Importantly, CQ is an applied concept. It is about translating information into knowledge and finally into action in the face of many, often competing, inputs. Indeed, "behave appropriately" is an easy concept to understand and yet a difficult one to implement, particularly as situations often arise in simultaneous, competing cultural spaces. Specifically, it is important to remember that CQ needs to be continuously applied with respect to the national, international and host-nation domains, as well as the antagonist/ enemy domain. (See Figure 4.) An understanding of all the players involved and how they see you is an important enabler in the COE.

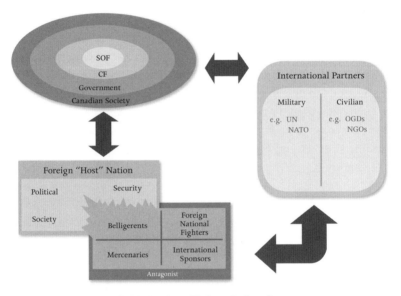

FIGURE 4.   Four CQ Domain Paradigm.

National Domain

Within the domestic realm there are a number of audiences that are critical for SOF to fully understand. The first is the Canadian general public, as public confidence and support is crucial to the continuing vitality of the CF and CANSOF. Additionally, a "cultural" comprehension of the Canadian public can have an impact on recruiting. Finally, understanding what is important to Canadians helps to prevent alienation, passivity or even active resistance particularly while assisting law enforcement agencies (LEAs) in a domestic context.

Another key domestic audience for SOF, and one for which CQ is especially important, is other governmental departments. In the contemporary and future operating environments, integrated operations are increasingly the norm. Personal relationships and trust are key in effectively working toward a common goal. Cultural understandings will help to remove suspicion and build credibility and trust, which often equates to freedom of action.

Importantly, CQ is also fundamental to achieving optimal cooperation between all CF elements. CQ can help build the foundations for cooperation, resource sharing, and operational support. It can also assist in recruiting the necessary individuals from the other services if SOF are seen as a partner and sister element vice a competitor or rival.

International Domain

The international benefit of CQ for SOF, whether dealing with allies, coalition partners, government agencies, international organizations or agencies, or non-governmental organizations follows a similar rationale, as already noted. Quite simply, understanding those you work with makes for smoother relationships, better communication and understanding, and, therefore, more effective operations.

As such, CQ is vital to the CANSOF task set of DDMA. Whenever training foreign or indigenous forces in counter-terrorism, internal defence, guerrilla warfare, or any form of security operations, understanding your audience is fundamental. What resonates with them? How do you get them to listen and fully participate? How do you develop bonds of trust and credibility? How do you appeal to their sense of duty and honour? How do you create lasting bonds of friendship and commitment?

In short, CQ is an important force multiplier for SOF in their relations and operations with international affiliates, both military and civilian. The proper utilization and application of CQ will enhance comprehension of, and communication with, our partners resulting in more effective outcomes.

Host-Nation Domain

Expressing CQ can help to generate support from the host-nation population, which has a direct impact on operations and assures that SOF are doing more good than harm. The support and cooperation of the population will create a more effective operating environment for friendly forces and deny the same to the enemy. Globally, expressing CQ can enhance force protection and reconstruction and development, while increasing information flow. Specifically, it can increase your ability to:

a. Provide information on adversary movements, identities and intentions;

b. Warn of adversary weapons and explosive caches, safe houses, ambush locations and Improvised Explosive Device (IED) placements;

c. Provide information on "communities" and define who belong and who do not; how authority and power are defined and codified; who are the power brokers and how resources are managed;

d. Provide information on key personalities, decision-makers and facilitators that can assist in mobilizing a target audience;

e. Define rules for interaction;

f. Explain relationships and social networks;

g. Provide information on local/regional atmospherics with regard to culture, economics, demographics, social issues;

h. Provide information on topographical issues such as best routes, environmental/ground limitations and restrictions;

i. Enhance cooperation and participation in development, governance and reconstruction initiatives;

j. Generate support and participation for local security initiatives; and

k. Increase overall support for national government and supporting coalition.

In sum, to win the support of the people, or in popular military jargon their "hearts and minds," it is critical to understand them. Specifically, it is essential that SOF operators be able to see through the eyes of the host-nation populace and comprehend how their own words, behaviours and actions are actually seen, interpreted and understood by the host-nation population. This ability requires detailed CQ.

Antagonist/Enemy Domain

With respect to the antagonist/enemy domain, applying CQ represents a valuable return on investment. Specifically, it can:

a. Provide insight into enemy motivation that could allow for diffusion of grievances or the co-opting of moderates;

b. Assist with debunking enemy information operations, propaganda and recruiting messages by highlighting discrepancies, contradictions and falsehoods;

c. Provide understanding of decision-making processes and value systems, thus, furnish possible weaknesses or stress points that can be manipulated;

d. Assist with the understanding of a pattern of behaviour that can provide insight into targeting (both the enemy's and your own), attack preferences (i.e. timing, locations, type, targets); likely reaction given situational circumstances (e.g. if faced with military or police actions), and normal pattern of life;

e. Assist with understanding history and symbology, which in turn provides insight into possible "safe areas" (sanctuary), historical and/or preferred attack positions/zones, targets and dates (i.e. historically, religiously or ideologically significant);

f. Provide insight into historic alliances and sponsors, which can lead to illuminating financing, supply nodes and routes, leadership engagements and possible sanctuaries; and

g. Provide insight into social networks, which in turn provide information on targeting of key personalities (i.e. leaders, facilitators, specialists) and intelligence gathering activities.

This list is not meant to be definitive. Rather, it is meant to highlight the types of information that can be obtained from applying CQ when analyzing the antagonist/enemy domain. A genuine understanding of the enemy as they see themselves – beyond our interpretation of their culture – will yield the greatest benefit in the struggle to vanquish our adversaries.

SUMMARY

Cultural Intelligence helps you see the world through different eyes. In so doing, it also enables you with the ability to reflect on how you are seen from this perspective. When working with people from diverse cultural backgrounds it is a very important tool to utilize to help ensure that the message that you are attempting to deliver is in the end the same message that is being received. No matter what the intent, at the end of the day, it is the actual impact that is important. As such, it is vital to ensure that your message is being delivered *and* received as you intend it to be so that it may be acted on accordingly.

NOTES

1   Notably, avoid overtly taking lots of notes when observing because for some it looks as if you are gathering information that you will later use against them. Note taking, particularly in a culture that does not commit much to paper, can be seen as assessing others, potentially negatively, for a report to their superiors. It tends to make individuals wary if not suspicious of your intent/purpose. If you need to write, be clear as to why and what you are recording.

2   Allan D. English, *Understanding Military Culture: A Canadian Perspective* (Montreal: McGill-Queen's University Press, 2004), 12. Notably, there is long-standing debate about the nature and definition of culture. The 2006 American counter-insurgency manual, for examples, contrasts cultural and social structures. It explains: "Social structure comprises the relationships among groups, institutions, and individuals within a society; in contrast, culture (ideas, norms, rituals, codes of behavior) provide meaning to individuals within the society." It defines culture as a "'web of meaning' shared by members of a particular society or group within a society." The manual explains this definition in terms of people's identity, beliefs, values, attitudes, perceptions and belief systems. It also emphasize that cultural knowledge about insurgents, as far as the military is concerned, should be exploited to be used to further U.S. national objectives. *Counterinsurgency*, 3-6, 3-8. Similarly, scholar Adam Bozeman, defines culture as "Those norms, values, institutions and modes of thinking in a given society that survive change and remain meaningful to successive generations." Adda Bozeman, cited in Montgomery McFate, "The Military Utility of Understanding Adversary Culture," *Joint Force Quarterly*, 38, 2005, 48, note 4. Additionally, sociologist Edgar Schein defines organizational culture, a concept that can be viewed much in the same way regional or national culture, as, "A pattern of basic assumptions, invented, discovered, or developed by a group as it learns to

cope with its problems of external adaptation and internal integration, that has worked well enough to be considered valid and, therefore, to be taught to new members as the correct way to perceive, think and feel in relation to those problems." E.H. Schein, *The Corporate Culture Survival Guide* (San Francisco, CA: Jossey-Bass Publishers, 1999), 9. In the end, Schein asserted that the essence of an organization's culture is its basic underlying assumptions, which are taken for granted by members. After all, he notes that these underlying assumptions "provide consistency for its members, order and structure, boundaries and ground rules, membership criteria, communication patterns, conditions for reward, punishment and the use of power." E.H. Schein, *Organizational Culture and Leadership*, 2nd Edition (San Francisco, CA: Jossey-Bass Publishers, 1992), 5. This process is understandable since organizational culture provides members with not only a sense of identity and belonging, but also with a set of unwritten, unspoken beliefs and norms of behaviour that regulate how members will get along with one another within a stable social system. While all these definitions (as well as most of the available definitions of culture) are complementary, English's does an exceptional job of breaking culture down into its component parts and thereby making the concept of culture more understandable at a structural level. For this reason, his definition is expanded on and returned to in discussions of culture.

3   Adapted from English, *Understanding Military Culture*, 12.

CHAPTER 9

EDUCATION:
A KEY ENABLER FOR SOF OPERATORS

COLONEL BERND HORN, PhD

Intuitively, virtually no-one would argue that more education is a bad thing. In fact, most would agree that, as a philosophical concept, the more education one has, the richer they are as a person. However, for special operations forces personnel, education is not "a nice to have," it is a critical enabler that empowers the SOF operator to be able to anticipate, adapt and change as required to meet the plethora of tasks and expectations facing SOF personnel in the ambiguous, chaotic, complex and volatile security environment of today and tomorrow. Moreover, in a world where building global partnerships is key, education becomes a critical enabler to success.

One need only examine the definition of SOF to begin to understand the nexus of education and special operations. After all, "Special Operation Forces are organizations containing specially selected personnel that are organized, equipped and trained to conduct high-risk, high value special operations to achieve military, political, economic or informational objectives by using special and unique operational methodologies in hostile, denied or politically sensitive areas to achieve desired tactical, operational and/or strategic effects in times of peace, conflict or war."[1] Fundamental to this definition and SOF effectiveness, is the fact that its strength lies in its people. SOF equip the operator rather than man the equipment. Selection and screening are fundamental principles of all SOF organizations. And, the individuals who are attracted to SOF, who volunteer and who are ultimately chosen to serve in SOF as a result of highly refined selection procedures and standards, are what provide the SOF edge – that is the key element for mission success.

It is this human interface, the in situ, instantaneous decision-making capability that is all powerful. And, it is fuelled and enhanced by continuous education. Furthermore, when one looks at the type of individuals SOF organizations seek, the importance of education becomes even more manifold. In short, SOF selects personnel who are:

1. *Risk Accepting* – individuals who are not reckless, but rather carefully consider all options and consequences and balance the risk of acting versus the failure to act. They possess the moral courage to make decisions and take action within the commander's intent and their legal parameters of action to achieve mission success.

2. *Creative* – individuals who are capable of assessing a situation and deriving innovative solutions, kinetic or non-kinetic to best resolve a particular circumstance. In essence, they have the intellectual and experiential ability to immediately change the combat process.

3. *Agile Thinkers* – individuals who are able to transition between tasks quickly and effortlessly. They can perform multiple tasks at the same time, in the same place with the same forces. They can seamlessly transition from kinetic to non-kinetic or vice versa employing the entire spectrum of military, political, social and economic solutions to complex problems to achieve the desired outcomes. They can react quickly to rapidly changing situations and transition between widely different activities and ensure they position themselves to exploit fleeting opportunities. Moreover, they can work effectively within rules of engagement in volatile, ambiguous and complex threat environments and use the appropriate levels of force.

4. *Adaptive* – individuals who respond effectively to changing situations and tasks as they arise. They do not fear the unknown and embrace change as an inherent and important, dynamic element in the evolution of organizations, warfare and society.

5. *Self-Reliant* – individuals who exercise professional military judgement and disciplined initiative to achieve the commander's intent without the necessity of constant supervision, support or encouragement. They accept that neither rank, nor appointment solely define responsibility for mission success. They function cohesively as part of a team but also perform superbly as individuals. They continue to carry on with a task until impossible to do so. They take control of their own professional development, personal affairs and destiny and ensure they strive to become the best possible military professional achievable. They demonstrate constant dedication, initiative and discipline and maintain the highest standards of personal conduct. They understand that they are responsible and accountable for their actions at all times and always make the correct moral decisions regardless of situation or circumstance.

6. *Eager for Challenge* – individuals who have an unconquerable desire to fight and win. They have an unflinching acceptance of risk and a mindset that accepts that no challenge is too great. They are tenacious, unyielding and unremitting in the pursuit of mission success.

7. *Naturally Orientated to the Pursuit of Excellence* – individuals who consistently demonstrate an uncompromising, persistent effort to excel at absolutely everything they do. Their driving focus is to attain the highest standards of personal, professional and technical expertise, competence and integrity. They have an unremitting emphasis on

continually adapting, innovating and learning to achieve the highest possible standards of personal, tactical and operational proficiency and effectiveness.

8. *Relentless in their Pursuit of Mission Success* – Individuals who embody a belief that first and foremost is service to country before self. They have an unwavering dedication to mission success and an acceptance of hardship and sacrifice. They strive to achieve mission success at all costs, yet within full compliance of legal mandates, civil law and the law of armed conflict.

9. *Culturally Attuned* – Individuals who are warrior-diplomats, who are comfortable fighting but equally skilled at finding non-kinetic solutions to problems. They are capable of operating individually, in small teams or larger organizations integrally, or with allies and coalition partners. They are also comfortable and adept at dealing with civilians, OGDs and international organizations, as well as NGOs. They are culturally attuned and understand that it is important to "see reality" through the eyes of another culture. They understand that it is not the message that was intended that is important but rather the message that was received that matters. They strive to be empathetic, understanding and respectful at all times when dealing with others. They comprehend that respect and understanding build trust, credibility and mission success.[2]

So, in light of such high quality personnel, the question often arises why is education such an important enabler? The answer is multifaceted. The immediate response must reference the contemporary operating environment, which is ambiguous, chaotic, complex, everchanging and extremely volatile. Moreover, if anything, it will become even more complex in the future. Globalization and persistent conflict, as well as the proliferation of cheap, accessible technology will continue to challenge the current understanding of conflict. Moreover, hybrid threats that include diverse combinations of irregular, terrorist, criminal, and conventional forces employed asymmetrically, all operating within populated centres in a variety of culturally diverse environments, are just some of the challenges that have added complexity to conflict.

In order to be effective in this environment, SOF must remain adaptive and agile in both thought and action. SOF personnel will need to be adept at critical thinking and sound reasoning – all benefits of education. In short, SOF requires warrior-scholars who are capable of operating in the complex battlespace of today and tomorrow.

Important to note at the outset is that training (as well as experience) are equally critical. However, education is normally subordinated to training and experience and much lesser attention given to its acquisition. This is not surprising since it is easy to understand why the military mind would focus on training and experience rather than education. After all, education is not tangible. Unlike training where quantifiable improvements in behaviour can be physically seen, for instance marksmanship scores or proficiency in drills, education is less evident in tangible form. It deals with creativity, critical thinking and reasoning.[3] These qualities are not always outwardly observable.

As such, there is a substantive difference between training and education. However, the traditional stress on training, that is "a predictable response to a predictable situation," is often confused with or considered synonymous with education, defined by Professor Ron Haycock as "the reasoned response to an unpredictable situation – critical thinking in the face of the unknown."[4] SOF's excellent training regime and its continuous success on operations makes it easy for individuals to be lulled into a perception that SOF's educational needs are quite adequately looked after. What is overlooked, at great peril, is that the prescribed application of ideas and methods, as well as drills and checklists, have a purpose and functional utility, but this methodology is no longer, if in fact it ever was, enough to equip leaders to cope with and function in the complex post-modern world.

Simply put, "education," according to Royal Military College of Canada (RMCC) Professor David Last, a former artillery senior officer, "is the shaping of the mind."[5] Education assists in our reasoning ability, which in turn is critical in responding to unanticipated circumstances. After all, as the adage goes, you train for certainty and educate for uncertainty. This is crucial to any and all SOF operators.

Equally important, is the need to understand, and ability to place, SOF operations within the context of the larger whole, particularly within the framework of the national interest and society SOF serves. The French emperor Napoleon Bonaparte already recognized in the 19th century that "Tactics, evolutions, artillery and engineer sciences can be learned from a manual like geometry; but the knowledge of the higher conduct of war can only be acquired by studying the history of wars and battles of great generals and by one's own experience." He understood, "There are no terse and precise rules at all."[6] In the end, neither the SOF, nor any of the components which make it up, exist in and of themselves.[7]

The requirement to comprehend the "the larger picture" cannot be understated.[8] Military professionals, asserts Professor Last, "are managers of violence." He further explains:

> Their professional education must allow them to understand it. Violence has always been a part of the interconnected human conditions that we label war, conflict, and peace. In the complex world of today and tomorrow, our understanding of these conditions needs to be more comprehensive than in the past. This is more important than technology, doctrine, and strategy,

because all are subservient to purpose. There is no purpose without understanding. The officer's understanding must match that of society – otherwise he or she cannot serve it.[9]

This societal connection has another, equally important, dimension. The Canadian Military Ethos demands that the Canadian Forces and by extension Canadian SOF remain rooted in Canadian society and reflect its most important values and attitudes. In this regard it is critical to understand that, as Ambassador Paul Heinbecker points out: "we are an extensively educated people."[10] Of the thirty-three most industrialized economies surveyed by the Organization for Economic Co-operation and Development (OECD), Canada ranked second behind Russia (Japan was third and the US fourth) in the percentage of the population that has attained at least a university or college-level education. The CF (and CANSOF) must remain very reflective of this leading edge sector of Canadian society if we are to retain the trust, confidence and respect necessary to maintain the essential support of all Canadian citizens.

In addition, the importance of education to the military profession, particularly in the post-modern world, as briefly mentioned already, should be self-evident. Intuitively, a professional soldier is better prepared to face the unknown challenges of the ambiguous, complex and uncertain battlespace by having a broad knowledge of theories that act as a guide to discretionary judgement rather than a narrow ability in only some of the practical applications of the profession of arms. As one expert concluded, "strategic effectiveness will increasingly be based on the capacity to think like a networked enemy. Therefore, the SOF operator needs to understand a complex environment and a diverse range of interests, actors and issues while retaining the capacity to "simplify, focus, decide and execute."[11] Retired American Major-General Robert H. Scales underlined the need for education vice training when he commented, "This new era of war requires soldiers equipped with exceptional cultural awareness and an intuitive sense for the nature and character of war."[12]

The need for education in today's complex security environment is repeatedly stressed by practitioners who through the experience in the chaos of conflict clearly understand that education, rooted in critical thinking, problem solving and analytical research, better prepares individuals to think, as well as cope with problems and situations that are unexpected. It assists individuals to not only embrace change, but adapt to and anticipate it. More importantly, it instills in people the attitude and ability to constantly learn from one's environment and to prepare, as well as react, accordingly. Colonel John Boyd stripped it down to its simplest form. He asserted, "Machines don't fight wars. Terrain doesn't fight wars. Humans fight wars." As such he concluded, "You must get in the minds of the humans. That's where the battles are won."[13]

And, education is the domain of the human mind. Sir Michael Howard wrote:

> ...academic studies can provide the knowledge, insight, and the analytic skills which provide the necessary basis, first for reasoned discussion, and then for action. They provide a forum, and breed the qualities, which enable the student, the teacher, the politician, the civil servant, the moral philosopher, and not least the soldier to reach a common understanding of the problems which confront them, even if inevitably there is disagreement about the solutions. This dialogue is what civilization is all about. Without it societies dissolve.[14]

Similarly, closer to home, Dr. John Cowan, the former Principal of RMCC, reinforced the necessity of education in relation to the military. He insisted that when a military professional is "called upon to be a skilled leader, a technical expert, a diplomat, a warrior, and even an interpreter and an aid expert all at once, there is no question that good training is not enough. Skills are not enough." Cowan added, "The job calls for judgement, that odd distillate of education, the thing which is left when the memorized facts have either fled or been smoothed into a point of view, the thing that cannot be taught directly, but which must be learned. Without the mature judgement which flows from education, we fall back on reflexes, which are damned fine things for handling known challenges, but which are manifestly unreliable when faced with new ones."[15]

Needless to say, as Cowan affirms, there will always be new challenges. This was reinforced by Lieutenant-General Andrew Leslie, a former deputy commander of the International Security Assistance Force in Afghanistan. "Individuals were sent home [from Afghanistan]," revealed Leslie, "Immaturity and the inability to actually think outside the box made them ineffective ... What they tried to do was bring their usually very limited experience from somewhere else and apply it the same way that it had been done somewhere else and that didn't work ... each mission has got it's own unique drivers, cultural conditions, local nuances, relationships with your other allies or other combatants."[16]

Leslie's observation is undisputable. Up until recently the common complaint of any deploying body was that they were prepared for the last deployment not the situation that they faced. Indeed, you don't know what you don't know. A culture absorbed solely by experience, whether in the former decades with a reliance on the 4 Canadian Mechanized Brigade Group (CMBG) experience of preparing to beat back the Soviet hordes at the Fulda Gap in Germany, or more currently on the Afghanistan experience of fighting the elusive Taliban in Kandahar Province, is oblivious to the value, if not necessity, of higher education.

Thankfully, General David Petraeus, accomplished soldier and veteran of years of combat in Iraq and a former commander of NATO forces in Afghanistan, supported the need for greater education, particularly graduate studies for senior officers. He affirmed "that a stint at graduate school takes military officers out of their intellectual comfort zones." Petraeus believed, "Such experiences are critical to the development of the flexible, adaptable, creative thinkers who are so important to operations in places like Iraq and Afghanistan."[17] He explained that "through such schooling our officers are often surprised to discover just how diverse and divergent views can be. We only thought we knew the contours of debate on a given subject."[18] Petraeus concluded that graduate studies "provide a fair amount of general intellectual capital and often provides specific skills and knowledge on which an officer may draw during his or her career."[19] Moreover, he argued, "graduate school inevitably helps U.S. military officers improve their critical thinking skills."[20]

A former Chief of the Defence Staff echoed these ideas. He insisted that military professionals "need to have the right mindset to change and evolve the profession." He added, "knowledge must be valued as a key ingredient to our growth as individuals and as a profession."[21] After all, as American General David Petraeus correctly identified, "The most powerful tool any soldier carries is not his weapon but his mind."[22]

In the end, every SOF member must ensure that they are ready to meet the challenges that face them not only today but also into the future. As such, education becomes a critical enabler to ensuring personnel are properly prepared. After all, many tenets of scholarship, namely precision, detailed research, communications, breadth of knowledge, placing events in a proper economic, political and social context, drawing conclusions and trying to discern themes there from, committing those to paper and then articulating them so that others can understand the argument put forward and learn from it, are all skills that are necessary for a SOF operator.

Equally important, this type of study provides vicarious experience. As already explained, experience is seen as sacrosanct and great emphasis is rightfully placed on it. But, due to real life limitations, experience is often constrained by time and place. Scholarship, on the other hand, allows its virtual experience to be timeless and cover a wider breadth of activity and circumstance. It provides soldiers with a greater repertoire of scenarios, possible solutions and context from which to draw.

And, as SOF ventures forth to develop global partnerships, these skills, attributes, attitudes and mindsets, will empower SOF operators to better understand, interact and work with others, particularly when working with unknown and alien cultures. Critical thinking skills, increased knowledge, enhanced tolerance and understanding will all facilitate more effective interaction with others. Clearly, education will endow SOF operators with greater knowledge confidence and critical thinking skills, which when combined with personal training and experience, will allow for greater probabilities of mission success regardless of circumstance.

In the end, education arms the SOF operator with the ability to deal with the ambiguity and complexity that our personnel face in the battlespace of today and tomorrow. Beyond the practical there is also the intangible. That is to say, a greater breadth of knowledge, tolerance to alternate interpretations and ideas, a comfort with critical debate and discussion, the honing of analytical skills, as well as the exposure to complete new bodies of literature and thought that expand the mind just make the SOF operator that much more capable. General Petraeus pronounced, "The future of the U.S. military requires that we be competent warfighters, but we cannot be competent warfighters unless we are as intelligent and mentally tough as we are aggressive and physically rugged."[23] It is no different for the Canadian Forces, particularly CANSOF.

NOTES

1   This is the official Canadian Special Operations Forces Command doctrinal definition. Canada, *CANSOFCOM Capstone Concept for Special Operations 2009* (Ottawa: DND, 2009), 4.

2   Ibid., 4.

3   "Creativity is critical requirement for adaptation. We need creativity because: When things change and new information comes into existence, it's no longer possible to solve current problems with yesterday's solutions. Over and over again, people are finding out that what worked two years ago won't work today. This gives them a choice. They can either bemoan the fact that things aren't as easy as they used to be, or they can use their creative abilities to find new answers, new solutions, and new ideas." Richard King, "How Stupid are We?," *Australian Army Journal* (Summer 2009), 186.

4   Dr. Ronald Haycock, former Dean of Arts, Royal Military College of Canada, "Clio and Mars in Canada: The Need for Military Education," presentation to the Canadian Club, Kingston, Ontario, 11 November 1999.

5   Major David Last, "Educating Officers: Post Modern Professionals to Control and Prevent Violence," in *Contemporary Issues in Officership: A Canadian Perspective*, ed. Lieutenant-Colonel Bernd Horn (Toronto: Canadian Institute of Strategic Studies, 2000), 26.

6   Cited in Murray Simons, *Professional Military Learning. Next Generation PME in the New Zealand Defence Force* (Canberra: Air Power Development Centre, 2004), 43.

7   This is why the US military believes that "successful operational adaptability depends upon educating and developing leaders, training soldiers, and building cohesive teams who are prepared to execute decentralized operations in and among populations in coordination with Joint, Interagency, Intergovernmental, Multinational (JIIMP) partners." United States of America, Department of the Army, *The Army Learning Concepts for 2015*. DRAFT. 20 April, 2010, 2.

8   Major-General Don McNamara asserted that advanced-military professional education is required "to get people to think in two ways. One, to think strategically so that they're not commanding a ship anymore, they're commanding a force, and that is a mindset that is not easy for a lot of people to change. The second thing is that they are now thinking in terms of dealing at the highest national levels and not at the level of an individual military formation. These are two major changes that are not easy for people to assume without getting some experience before they actually have to assume it." Don Macnamara in John Wood (ed.), *Talking Heads Talking Arms: No Life Jackets* (Toronto: Breakout Educational Network, 2003), 155.

9   Ibid., 9.

10   Paul Heinbecker, *Getting Back in the Game: A Foreign Policy Playbook for Canada* (Toronto: Key Porter Books, 2010), 23.

11   Colonel Roger Noble, "'Beyond Cultural Awareness': Anthropology as an Aid to the Formulation and Execution of Military Strategy in the Twenty-First Century," *Australian Army Journal*, (winter 2009), 67.

12   Cited in Emily Spencer, *Solving the People Puzzle: Cultural Intelligence and Special Operations Forces* (Toronto: Dundurn Press, 2010), 115.

13   Colonel John R. Boyd, (USAF Ret) cited in Major Jason Hayes, "Preparing Our Soldiers for Operations within Complex Human Terrain Environments," *Australian Army Journal*, (winter 2009), 104.

14   Michael Howard, *The Causes of War* (New York: Harvard University Press, 1984), 83.

15   Dr. John Scott Cowan, RMCC Convocation Address, 4 October 1999, Kingston, Ontario. See also Eliot Cohen and John Gooch, *Military Misfortunes. The Anatomy of Failure in War* (New York: Vintage Books, 1991), 233-237.

16   Cited in Spencer, 72.

17   David H. Petraeus, "To Ph.D. or Not to Ph.D...." *The American Interest* (July/August 2007), 16.

18   Ibid., 18. He further insists, "This is a very valuable experience in and of itself for those of us in uniform who will work and live in other cultures overseas. If the range of views within our own country is greater than we supposed, that can only help prepare officers for an even wider range beyond our shores."

19   Ibid., 18.

20   Ibid., 19.

21   Lieutenant-General M.K. Jeffery, address to the Commanding Officers Course 2001, 21 June 2001, Fort Frontenac, Kingston, Ontario.

22   Petraeus, 16.

23   Ibid., 20.

CHAPTER 10

PHYSICAL FITNESS FOR THE BRAIN: SELLING EDUCATION

DR. EMILY SPENCER

The stereotypical public image, albeit not necessarily correct, of a special operations forces operator is that of an athletic, muscular male who has generally not maintained the military standards of dress and decorum and who instead has replaced the conventional norm with a cooler-than-cool like appearance that ironically makes him easily identifiable. The rationalization is of course that SOF's special selection, skills and missions demand an alienation from the norm for reasons of secrecy and the requirement for extreme physical prowess. This image is reflective of a 21st century Rambo – an individual who is singularly capable of dealing with any situation that is thrown at him and whose method of conflict resolution is generally physical in nature.

Notably, this stereotype, while incomplete, is not necessarily a polarization of reality. While there is no gender discrimination for SOF in Canada, the majority of operators are male. Also, the physical demands of the training and the missions often create very muscularly defined individuals. Moreover, partially for necessity and philosophical inclination, there generally is a relaxed attitude toward military decorum, both dress and behaviour.

Importantly though, there is much more to the SOF story. In particular, not all SOF activities are kinetic in nature. In fact, when you examine the list of SOF tasks it may be surprising to realize that many rely on non-kinetic skills, with force being used only as a last resort.[1] Additionally, as much as physical attributes can help with selection and training, cognitive and psychological traits are

equally significant in selection and training and, more importantly, to mission success. Finally, SOF rarely operate alone and instead
rely on their fellow SOF members as well as conventional forces.

Nonetheless, many individuals are drawn to SOF because of the
mystique that surrounds such organizations and the perceived
physicality of the job. In this scenario, the gym and firing range
are often the proving-ground rather than the classroom; "education" is decidedly second to "training" as the former is seen to
rely on the academic and abstract whereas the latter is believed
as essential to providing practical skill-sets that will contribute to
personal survival and mission success.

However, in a world where good thinking and communications
skills are increasingly required for all military personnel in order
for them to achieve a desired effect in a complex and ambiguous
contemporary operating environment, education is increasingly
critical. In fact, it is now essential that it be fully integrated into
the training cycle. This is a particularly valid point for SOF whose
members are already selected for their creativity, adaptability and
ability to be agile thinkers among other things, but who can nonetheless always improve on these skills. Arguably, even more so
than for other military members, SOF will be required to use these
"softer" skills in an operational context where tactical actions may
have strategic implications. As such, the importance of an effective education combined with training in these softer skill-sets
is paramount for success in the contemporary and future operating environments. It is thus vital to have education applied in the
training environment.

DEFINING EDUCATION AND TRAINING

It is first necessary to distinguish between education and training,
two distinct terms that nonetheless are sometimes used inter-
changeably. As Ron Haycock, a professor at the Royal Military
College of Canada explained, training provides "a predictable

response to a predictable situation." On the other hand, education provides individuals with the ability to come up with a "reasoned response to an unpredictable situation — critical thinking in the face of the unknown."[2]

There are undoubtedly benefits to both education and training for military members. Colonel Bernd Horn, also affiliated with the RMCC, is clear in his explanation of the benefits of a "soldier/ scholar." He surmised, "A greater breadth of knowledge, tolerance to alternate interpretations and ideas, familiarity with critical debate and discussion, the honing of analytical skills, as well as the exposure to complete new bodies of literature and thought expand the mind and make the soldier that much more capable.... For far too long these two entities have remained apart when in fact they should be fused to strengthen both disciplines."[3]

At this point, it is important to clarify that education should not be restricted to meaning an institutionalized education in a formal schooling environment. Education as defined by Haycock as "learning to apply a reasoned response to an unpredictable situation" can be learned in any environment and is not dependent on a certificate of achievement. Unlike the scarecrow in the *Wizard of Oz* who is thought not to have a brain until he receives a diploma (although, arguably, author L. Frank Baum is simply underscoring the irony of such associations), being educated and having the ability to think, respond and adapt to any situation quickly and effectively has nothing to do with academic letters of achievement. In fact, some people who hold degrees may in the end be poorly educated, as education is defined in this paper and, conversely, many individuals who lack the academic credentials may in the end be highly educated.

Notably, these comments should not be taken as a slight on academics. Indeed, academic courses and programs are designed to enhance one's ability to form a reasoned response to an unpredictable situation and in so doing improve thinking, self-awareness, cultural intelligence and strategic communication skills, which, as will be argued, are pillars for success in the COE. Additionally, academic programs are purposefully designed to systematically build on these skills through increased knowledge in the field, with introductory courses providing the basics in any given field and advanced courses and post-graduate courses increasingly building on this understanding and knowledge.

As such, the debate should truly no longer be about the benefits of an education for military members – something that is clearly an undeniable asset and force multiplier in the contemporary operating environment.[4] Rather, the focus should now be on what should be taught and how this knowledge can be most effectively transmitted in order to have an applied effect in the operational world. In order to provide an answer to this complex query, this chapter proposes a five-step plan for improving the calibre of SOF personnel through a combination of education and training in softer skill-sets.

STEP 1: DEMONSTRATE THE IMPORTANCE OF EDUCATION TO SUCCESS IN THE CONTEMPORARY OPERATING ENVIRONMENT

Thinking is a process that we do everyday and, like breathing, we are sometimes conscious of it and more often than not we take it for granted. Often when you behave in a careless or inappropriate way, the reasoning, or more appropriately the excuse, is that you were "not thinking." The reality is, however, that you were thinking, you simply were not doing so effectively.

Like an elite athlete who learns to control his or her breathing in order to maximize output, one's ability to think more effectively can be practiced and improved upon. Importantly, with improved thinking comes improved decision-making. Ultimately, improved decision-making allows one to more successfully and quickly determine the best course of action (COA) under potentially dynamic, complex and stressful situations. The benefits to SOF of improved thinking are thus clearly observable.

Notably, there is a direct link between education (as defined in this paper) and improved thinking. As a general rule, the more educated one is, the better his or her thinking becomes.[5]

Education, or that ability to perform a "reasoned response to an unpredictable situation," requires even further explanation at this point. First, it should be noted that education should not be considered merely the transmission of knowledge and skills from "teacher" to "student", or simply the accumulation of "fact". Rather a more holistic approach should be applied to the term "education" by which an education is seen as the process of gaining knowledge and, more importantly, the ability to assess and use this knowledge to achieve a desired end state. In this way, an education is more about *how* to think than *what* to think.

A schooling in how to break issues down into their component parts – often referred to as critical thinking – and how to come up with diverse potential solutions – meaning creative thinking – should be at the core of educational goals for SOF personnel. By combining these two elements, which have sometimes been lumped under the term "strategic thinking", with emotional thinking, that third element that is generally omnipresent in the thought process, it is possible to practice and improve decision-making.[6]

There is no doubt that improved decision-making can contribute to achieving a desired strategic effect in the COE, particularly for SOF. For example, a veteran of the war in Afghanistan noted that he was stunned following a night raid when an Afghan came up to him and suggested that he would prefer the coalition forces kill one of his kids rather than his dog, an issue that had arisen because dogs were being shot during nocturnal operations when they would bark, thereby potentially alerting the Taliban to the location of coalition forces. The veteran was astounded. All he heard was: "kill my kid rather than my dog." Given the way that Afghans treat their dogs, which is in stark contrast to many of the pampered pooches in the West, the sentiment seemed even more unconscionable to the Canadian. While there was an understanding that winning Afghan "hearts and minds" was part of their mission, the Afghan's declaration simply alienated the Canadian's trust and respect for the locals.

Now the issue could simply be left alone and a determination could be reached on whether or not winning the hearts and minds of locals was worth the associated risk of having dogs bark during night raids. Alternatively, an educated person might explore the issue more deeply.

In Afghanistan, dogs are considered working animals and a well-trained dog is an asset for farming and essential for protection. Moreover, well-trained dogs are hard to come by. Additionally, the country is faced with one of the highest infant mortality rates and death rates. As such, perhaps the Afghan was not really saying that he would rather one of his kids were killed instead of his dog. It is quite plausible that he instead was trying to communicate the severe implications of killing the dogs, that being that by killing their dogs the coalition forces were directly hurting the Afghans' ability to survive. In fact, this is a completely different message than what was heard and understood by the Canadian veteran. This new communication is one that many Canadian Forces members would deem important to act on: please stop hindering our chances of survival.

Additionally, having applied critical thinking skills to determine what the issue was actually about, it is then much less challenging to apply those creative thinking skills to determine what potential solutions exist. For instance, recordings of barking dogs could be placed as decoys, tranquilizer darts could be used or compensation could be provided when a dog had to be killed, just to mention a few possible COAs. The point is that you have to really understand the problem first in order to apply the necessary resources, including time and energy, to come up with creative solutions.

Far too often it is easiest to just take information at perceived face value and act accordingly. It is much more challenging to dissect information in order to uncover its true meaning. An education that extends beyond the mere accumulation of facts and knowledge and which perfects the mechanism of how to think greatly facilitates one's ability to analyze information. This one example illustrates how an educated view can provide a different perception on issues and lead to different COAs than simply taking information at face value. Notably, these different COAs could have drastically different strategic effects, with the educated decision generally leading to the more desired strategic end.

Simply because one is educated does not mean that an individual will always make good decisions but it does increase the potential for good decision-making. As this one example indicates, an education in how to think can help you understand the actual intent of messages more clearly and thus be able to act in a more appropriate manner in order to achieve your goals. As determining the best COA to have a desired strategic effect is paramount to many SOF missions, the benefits of an education, which inevitably improves the ability in how to think more effectively, are thus transparent. Moreover, as this volume underscores, as SOF missions increasingly move into the realm of defence, development and military assistance type tasks, the requirements to understand and communicate effectively will be even more central to mission success and thereby further underscore the importance of education for SOF.

STEP 2: HAVE THE LEADERSHIP BUY-INTO THE REQUIREMENT

It is easy to espouse the value of education for SOF members, however, in order to achieve the goal of increasing the education of SOF personnel, leadership at the formation, unit and sub-unit levels need to have actively and philosophically embraced and inculcated this concept. There is no doubt that Canadian Special Operations Forces seek individuals who are creative, adaptive and agile thinkers but it is important to remember that these skills need to be continuously practiced and challenged in order to be simply maintained, let alone improved on.

At the command level, the value that is attributed to education is clear. In 2009, the Canadian Special Operations Command germinated the idea, and began to create, a CANSOFCOM Professional Development Centre (PDC). It was officially stood-up in 2010 with the mission to enable professional development within the command in order to continually develop and enhance the cognitive capacity of CANSOFCOM personnel. Specifically, the CANSOFCOM PDC is designed to provide CANSOFCOM additional capacity to:

1. develop the cognitive capacity of CANSOFCOM personnel;

2. access subject matter advice on diverse subjects from the widest possible network of scholars, researchers, subject matter experts (SMEs), institutions and organizations;

3. provide additional research capacity;

4. develop educational opportunities and SOF specific courses and professional development materials;

5. record the classified history of CANSOFCOM;

6. develop CANSOF publications that provide both professional development (PD) and educational materials to CANSOF personnel and external audiences

7. maintain a website that provides up-to-date information on PD opportunities and research materials; and

8. assist with the research of SOF best practices and concepts to ensure that CANSOFCOM remains relevant and progressive so that it maintains its position as the domestic force of last resort and the international force of choice for the Government of Canada.

Each of CANSOFCOM's four units (Joint Task Force 2, Canadian Joint Incident Response Unit, Canadian Special Operations Regiment and 427 Special Operations Aviation Squadron), as well as the Headquarters, has the ability to request support directly from the PDC and access Command-wide education initiatives that the PDC provides. The fact that the PDC is a widely used resource again speaks to the value associated with education throughout the Command. Additionally, these resources are often accessed at the sub-unit level even further underscoring the value associated with these educational initiatives.

Despite the overwhelming positive feedback and use of PDC resources, there remain two important areas in which CANSOF leadership could further advance the education of its forces. First, while remaining adaptable and agile, certain professional development briefs should become "must have" requirements, rather than "nice to have" educational opportunities. Second, for education to be more formalized in this manner achievement needs to count toward advancement, as well as increased responsibility and appointment.

To make sure that all CANSOF members have a base-line education it is important that certain cognitive PD briefs are offered regularly and become mandatory benchmarks rather than being left to the discretion of individuals in certain positions. Akin to basic training skills, this standardization would ensure that all CANSOF personnel would reach a minimum educational level that could then be built on depending on requirements. Notably, these educational PD briefs would not necessarily be for external credit (i.e. university credit courses) but to be taken seriously they would need to be formally recognized and potentially count toward advancement as previously discussed. What is comes down to is that time and effort needed to be directed toward educational opportunities, whether in the form of academic courses or non-credit PD briefs, and members need to clearly see the links between achievements in these areas and success in their careers and on missions.

STEP 3: IDENTIFY AND PRIORITIZE
EDUCATIONAL GOALS

Time is one of the most valuable assets as it is non-replenishable and generally in short supply, something that is overwhelmingly true for CANSOF personnel. As such, if members are going to dedicate their time, as well as other resources, to education, then the benefits of these commitments needs to be obvious. To help achieve this goal there needs to be a sound determination of what skills need to be taught and why.

As mentioned, enhanced thinking and communications skills are paramount to success in the COE and will more than likely continue to be for future operating environments. Consequently, education should focus on these two areas and include strategic thinking, self-awareness, cultural intelligence and strategic communications as the building blocks of creating better thinking and communication skills. In this way, a solid foundation can be built of the following four skill-sets: how to think; how you see yourself and how others might see you; how you see others and how they might see themselves; and how you can communicate effectively so as to achieve your desired goal.

By setting up PD sessions on strategic thinking, self-awareness, cultural intelligence and strategic communications, CANSOF would be providing the foundation for cognitive success in the COE. This is not to say that education should be limited to these four areas of inquiry. Rather, while all education should be considered valuable, for SOF personnel it is how education strengthens those pillars that will determine its value to missions.

In the end, SOF personnel need to know how to think and communicate effectively. In addition to strategic thinking and communication, self-awareness and cultural intelligence will help them achieve these goals. As such, PD sessions in these areas should be readily available and not just considered nice-to-have items but rather must-have ones.

Education should not end here, however. The pursuit of learning and knowledge should be encouraged through the pursuit of higher education and additional PD sessions. Although it has been argued that too much education could be a detriment to military members as it might slow their reaction time,[7] it is much more arguable that the more educated a person is – the more adept they are at coming up with a reasoned response to an unpredictable situation – the more effective they will be in the COE. That is not to say that education should take the place of training that provides operators with the ability to react quickly and effectively in a crisis or emergency situation. Instead, education helps to assure that they apply the correct trained response in any given situation. Rather than slow reaction time, education makes you more aware of your environment and able to predict and respond to change. As such, it helps build cognitive adaptability, which is crucial for SOF personnel.

STEP 4: IDENTIFY WHICH SKILL-SETS ARE REQUIRED FOR WHICH INDIVIDUALS

Akin to physical training, cognitive skills improve with use and deteriorate when they are not being applied regularly. As such, all cognitive PD sessions and other educational opportunities should be continuously developed within members. Given that this process takes time, however, and time is a very limited resource, it is worthwhile to consider which ranks and trades will benefit most from these resources.

Unlike the larger CF that tends to prefer an education for officers or non-commissioned officers over all members, CANSOFCOM needs to fully recognize that an education is important for all its members regardless of commission or rank. Not only do many tactical actions have strategic consequences during SOF missions – as they are designed specifically to do – but there is also the reality of the phenomenon of the "strategic corporal" whereby any action by any individual when captured by a virtually omnipresent media can also have strategic consequences. As such, a baseline of education in strategic thinking, self-awareness, cultural intelligence and strategic communications should be established for CANSOF personnel. Moreover, these skills should be updated regularly as they will improve with practice and can disappear when not used.

Beyond this baseline, which really underscores the processes of how to think and communicate effectively, more focused educational needs can be determined based on rank, trade or mission. Importantly, once a baseline is established it will be easier for members to incorporate additional education into useful skill-sets that can be applied on operations. In this way, education should be considered a lifelong process that should be continuously updated in order for cognitive skills to be maintained and enhanced.

STEP 5: INTEGRATE EDUCATION INTO THE TRAINING ENVIRONMENT (WHERE THE CLASSROOM MEETS THE PAVEMENT)

Even when education is valued within the military, it is often separated from training. Education – the development of cognitive skills in order to be able to apply a reasoned response to an unpredictable situation – is still for the most part considered superfluous to training, which most military personnel believe is where you will learn the skills that will contribute to survival and mission success. Rarely are the benefits of sitting in a classroom, reading a book or studying material directly tied to one's ability to perform in the COE and thus education for many remains a "nice to have" rather than a "must have."

Part of the problem is that education is still for the most part separated from training whereas the reality of the COE demands that both skill-sets are applied simultaneously. It is not enough that you can determine an effective COA in a pedagogical environment where you are physically comfortable and where time is of little relevance. What is important for CF members, and CANSOF personnel in particular, is that you can determine the best COA in potentially volatile and dynamic situations, under physically challenging conditions and severe time constraints. If we ask individuals to apply cognitive, psychological and physical skills simultaneously in complex, potentially hazardous situations, we should be integrating these skill-sets into combined education and training exercises beforehand. For SOF, it is not enough to be good at strategic thinking and communicating; you need to be good at these skills when pushed to your physical limit, pressed for time and in a hostile environment.

Clearly, education and training need to fit together. By taking education out of the classroom and integrating it within training you not only underscore the value of education to success during operations, you also create a more real-life learning environment that is more likely to appeal to the individuals who choose a career path in the CF and CANSOF in particular than a standardized classroom environment.

CONCLUSION

A central reason for why extreme fitness is important for SOF operators is that this state of physical conditioning allows them to think while a "normal" person would be overcome by the physical circumstances. Consequently, it only makes sense that your mind is as prepared as your body for operations. As such, education, particularly enhanced strategic thinking and communication skills, needs to be continuously developed among SOF personnel. Regular PD sessions on strategic thinking, self-aware-ness, cultural intelligence and strategic communications will help build the foundation for establishing these softer cognitive skills. Importantly, since we are not asking operators to "think" and "act" under different circumstances, we should not separate the education and training environments.[8] An integrated approach to education and training will help to underscore their importance to one another and to success in the contemporary and future operating environments.

NOTES

1   "Non-Kinetic" options refer to a wide range of skills and task sets that include provision of strategic advisory teams, defence, development and military assistance, information operations, psychological opera-tions, and support to other military, paramilitary or law enforcement agencies.

2   Ronald Haycock, cited in Bernd Horn, "Soldier/Scholar: An Ir-reconcilable Divide?" *The Army Doctrine and Training Bulletin*, Vol 4, No. 4, Winter 2001–2002, 4.

3   Ibid., 7.

4   Interestingly, however, there is still some debate on this issue. In "Warrior Wisdom: To PhD or Not," David H. Petraeus argues strongly for the need for education amongst military professionals. In fact, he be-gins by stating that "the most powerful tool any soldier carries is not his weapon but his mind." In the same article, however, Ralph Peters argues that too much thinking can slow decision-making and be a detriment to the profession of arms. He remarks that "wars are won by officers who know the smell of the streets, not by those who swoon over political science texts." Arguably, however, even Peters could be persuaded of the benefits of education as defined in this paper. For further elabora-tion on this topic see also Bernd Horn "Education: A Key Enabler for SOF Operators" in this volume. David H. Petraeus and Ralph Peters,

"Warrior Wisdom: To PhD or Not," *The American Interest*, July/August 2007, 16-28, quotes 16 and 24.

5   It should be noted that the scale is per individual and does not necessarily apply between individuals. For example, Sarah might have no education but be naturally quite good at thinking and thus better than John who has a lot of education. John, however, will be better at thinking once he has received an education than he was before he received an education.

6   Interestingly, it is now being argued that medical doctors need to enhance their critical thinking skills (the how to think part) over simply the accumulation of fact. The argument rests on the idea that increasing critical thinking among doctors will help to minimize the occurrence of medical mistakes. For a summary of this debate see Rachel Giese, "The Errors of Their Ways," *The Walrus*, April 2012, 24-32.

7   Ralph Peters in David H. Petraeus and Ralph Peters, "Warrior Wisdom: To PhD or Not".

8   Inded, Geoff Peterson makes it clear when he states that the purpose of professional military education is to "develop strategic leaders who can 'think then do'." Geoff Peterson, "Nurturing the Australian Military Mind: A Considered Assessment of Senior Professional Military Education," *Centre for Defence and Strategic Studies Australian Defence College*, March 2012, 10-11.

CONTRIBUTORS

Dr. Howard G. Coombs retired from active duty with the Canadian Forces in 2003. He is a graduate of the Canadian Forces Staff School, Canadian Land Force Command and Staff College, United States Army Command and General Staff College, and the US Army School of Advanced Military Studies, which awarded his Master's degree. Coombs received his PhD in military history from Queen's University in Kingston, Ontario and is currently an Assistant Professor of the Royal Military College of Canada. He is also a part-time reserve officer who commands 33 Canadian Brigade Group, headquartered in Ottawa. Coombs deployed with Joint Task Force Afghanistan from September 2010 to July 2011 as a civilian advisor to the Task Force Commander

Colonel Bernd Horn is an experienced infantry officer who has has filled key command appointments such as the Deputy Commander Canadian Special Operations Forces Command, Commanding Officer of the 1st Battalion, The Royal Canadian Regiment and Officer Commanding 3 Commando, the Canadian Airborne Regiment. Dr. Horn is also an Adjunct Professor of History at the Royal Military College of Canada and Norwich University. He has authored, co-authored, edited and co-edited in 35 books and over 100 chapters and articles on military history and military affairs.

Dr. William (Bill) Knarr serves as a resident senior fellow with the Joint Special Operations University (JSOU) Strategic Studies Department. Dr. Knarr came to JSOU from the Institute for Defense Analyses where he worked as a project leader/researcher. Prior to that, Dr. Knarr served in the US Army, retiring as a colonel in 2002. Dr. Knarr has a Doctorate in Education, Master's degrees in Systems Management and National Security Strategy, and a Bachelor of Science in Mathematics. His military education includes the Air Command and Staff College and the National War College.

US Brigadier-General (Retired) Hector Pagan is a graduate of the Infantry Officer Basic and Advanced Courses, the Combined Arms and Services Staff School, the Special Forces Detachment Officer Qualification Course, the Army Command and General Staff Course, the Joint Forces Staff College and the Army War College. He earned a Master's degree in management from Troy State University and a Master's degree in strategic studies from the U.S. Army War College. Brigadier-General Pagan served as the deputy commander, U.S. Army Special Operations Command in November 2006 and in May 2007 assumed duties as deputy commander, U.S. Army John F. Kennedy Special Warfare Center at Fort Bragg, North Carolina until July, 2008. Brigadier-General Pagan commanded the Special Operations Command South from July 18, 2008 to September 2010 where he was in charge of Special Operations Forces deployments in Latin America.

David Pugliese, an award winning journalist, covers military issues for the *Ottawa Citizen*. His freelance articles on military issues have also appeared in more than a dozen publications. Additionally, he is author of two best-selling books on special operations forces. Pugliese's assignments in the field have ranged from taking part in a mission on board a Strategic Air Command B-52 bomber to submarine operations on HMCS *Victoria* and HMCS *Windsor* to chronicling the training of the Canadian Special Operations Regiment and the Canadian Special Operations Forces Command's joint nuclear, biological and chemical warfare unit.

Colonel Mike Rouleau was commissioned as a Field Artillery Officer in 1986. In 1999, then-Major Rouleau released from the CF to join the Ottawa Police Service as an Emergency Response Officer. Following the events of 9-11, he re-enrolled into the CF in 2002 serving again in JTF 2, this time as the Chief Instructor. In 2004 he became the Second in Command of 5ᵉ Régiment d'artillerie légère du Canada before being recalled to Ottawa to serve on CDS Action Team 2 (Force Generation) as a SOF Representative in the time of General Rick Hillier's Transformation. He attended Command

and Staff College in 05-06 and immediately following Staff College deployed to Afghanistan as a Special Operations Task Force Commander in 2006/07 where he was awarded the Meritorious Service Cross in recognition of what his troops accomplished. Colonel Rouleau became the Commanding Officer of Joint Task Force 2 in May 2007, a position he held until June 2009 whereupon he attended the National Security Program at the Canadian Forces College in 2009/10. He was Army Commander Lieutenant-General Devlin's Executive Assistant until June 2010 and on promotion, became Director Capability Integration within Chief of Force Development, a position he occupies today. He also serves CANSOFCOM as the Director of Special Operations Forces as a secondary portfolio.

Dr. Emily Spencer is the Director Research and Education at the CANSOFCOM Professional Development Centre. She holds a PhD in War Studies from the Royal Military College of Canada and has authored/co-authored or edited numerous books, chapters and articles on the contemporary operating environment. Her research focuses on the importance of cultural knowledge to success in the contemporary operating environment, as well as the role the media plays in shaping understandings of world events.

Brigadier-General Denis Thompson joined the Militia as a Private in 1978 and entered the Collège militaire royale de St-Jean in 1979. In 1984, he graduated from the Royal Military College of Canada at Kingston and served with the 3rd Battalion, The Royal Canadian Regiment in Winnipeg, Cyprus and Germany. From 1992 to 1995 he served as the Training Officer for Joint Task Force 2. Upon promotion to Major in 1995, he was posted to the 2nd Battalion, The Royal Canadian Regiment as Officer Commanding G Company, leading them as part of the Queen's Royal Hussars Battle Group on the initial NATO mission in Bosnia. In 1998, Brigadier-General Thompson was appointed the Deputy Commanding Officer of the 1st Battalion, afterward joining Headquarters 2 Canadian Mechanized Brigade Group as the G3. In June 2000, Brigadier-General Thompson assumed command of the 3rd Battalion,

The Royal Canadian Regiment deploying with them in 2001 as the Battle Group Commander in Bosnia. On leaving Regimental duty in July 2002, he took up a post as a policy officer including a secondment to DFAIT, departing in January 2005 as the Director of Peacekeeping Policy. In June 2006, Brigadier-General Thompson was appointed Brigade Commander of 2 Canadian Mechanized Brigade Group in Petawawa until assuming command of ISAF's Task Force Kandahar in Afghanistan from May 2008 to February 2009. Since then, he has served in a number of staff positions at National Defence Headquarters, until his appointment as Commander of Canadian Special Operations Command in April 2011.

Lieutenant-Colonel John Vass graduated from the Royal Military College of Canada with a Bachelor of Science degree in 1994 after which he was posted to the 1st Battalion and then 3rd Battalion, The Royal Canadian Regiment in Petawawa, Ontario. Holding a variety of positions within both battalions, he also deployed on a UN mission to Croatia and a NATO mission to Bosnia during his regimental tours. Following a two-year posting to Borden in 2000 as the Executive Assistant to the Commander of the Canadian Forces Support Training Group and the completion of the Transition Command and Staff College at the CLFCSC in Kingston, Lieutenant-Colonel Vass returned to the 3rd Battalion as the Adjutant. After his promotion to Major in December 2002, he was privileged to command Parachute Company, which included an operational tour on Operation ATHENA, Roto 0 in Afghanistan where he was awarded a Mention in Dispatches. Leaving 3rd Battalion as the Deputy Commanding Officer, he moved to Fort Leavenworth, Kansas to complete the US Army Command and General Staff Course and attain his Master's in Military Arts and Sciences. Upon return to Canada in January 2008, Lieutenant-Colonel Vass became the Chief of Operations for the Canadian Special Operations Regiment. On promotion to his current rank in June 2009, he moved to CANSOFCOM Headquarters as the Command J7 and was appointed the Commanding Officer of CSOR in June 2010.

GLOSSARY OF ABBREVIATIONS

3D+C	Defence, diplomacy, development plus commerce
9/11	11 September 2001
AAR	After Action Report
ADM–POL	Associate Deputy Minister – Policy
AFRICOM	Africa Command
ALP	Afghanistan Local Police
ANA	Afghanistan National Army
ANASOC	Afghan National Army Special Operations Command
ANP	Afghanistan National Police
ANSF	Afghan National Security Forces
AO	Area of Operation
APEC	Asia-Pacific Economic Cooperation
AQUIM	Al-Qaeda in the Islamic Maghreb
ASEAN	Association of Southeast Asian Nations
ASG	Afghan Security Guards
C4ISR	Command, control, communications, computers, intelligence, surveillance and reconnaissance
CANSOF	Canadian Special Operations Forces
CANSOFCOM	Canadian Special Operations Forces Command
CCTM-A	Canadian Contribution Training Mission – Afghanistan
CDS	Chief of Defence Staff
CEFCOM	Canadian Expeditionary Force Command
CF	Canadian Forces
CFDS	Canada First Defence Strategy

CIDA	Canadian International Development Agency
CIMIC	Civil-Military Cooperation
CLS	Chief of the Land Staff
CMBG	Canadian Mechanized Brigade Group
CMR	Civil Military Relations
COA	Course of action
COE	Contemporary operating environment
COIN	Counter-insurgency
Comd RC(S)	Commander Regional Command South
COP	Combat Outpost
CQ	Cultural Intelligence
CSOR	Canadian Special Operations Regiment
CT	Counter-terrorism
DDMA	Defence, Diplomacy, and Military Assistance
DFAIT	Department of Foreign Affairs and International Trade
DMTC	Directorate of Military Training and Cooperation
DND	Department of National Defence
DO	Defence objectives
FID	Foreign Internal Defense
FMLN	Farabundo Martí National Liberation Front
FOBs	Forward Operating Bases
GCC	Gulf Co-operation Council
GDP	Gross domestic product
GIRoA	Government of the Islamic Republic of Afghanistan
GoC	Government of Canada
HMMWV	High Mobility Multipurpose Wheeled Vehicle
HN	Host Nation
HVTs	High value tasks

IED	Improvised Explosive Device
IO	Information Operations
IO	International Organizations
IOC	Initial Operationa Capability
ISAF	International Security Assistance Force
ISR	Inteligence Surveillance Reconnaissance
JDF	Jamaica Defence Force
JIMP	Joint, International, Multi-Agency and Public
JSOU	Joint Special Operations University
JTF 2	Joint Task Force 2
KPRT	Kandahar Provincial Reconstruction Team
LEA	Law enforcement agencies
MARSOC	Marine Corps Special Operations Command
MASC	Military Assistance Steering Committee
MISO	Military Information Support Operations
MND	Minister of National Defence
MoI	Ministry of Interior
MSF	Malian Security Forces
MTCP	Military Training and Cooperation Program
MTT	Mobile training team
NATO	North Atlantic Treaty Organization
NCM	Non-commissioned Member
NCO	Non-commissioned Officer
NDHQ	National Defence Headquarters
NGO	Non-governmental Organizations
NORAD	North American Aerospace Defence Command
NTM-A	NATO Training Mission Afghanistan
NVGs	Night vision goggles
ODA	Operational Detachment Alpha
OECD	Organization for Economic Co-operation and Development

OGD/A	Other government departments and agencies
OPSEC	Operations security
PDC	Professional Development Centre
PD	Professional development
PRC	Provincial Response Company
PRC-K	Provincial Response Company – Kandahar
PSO	Peace Support Operations
PSYOPs	Psychological Operations
QRF	Quick Reaction Force
RCMP	Royal Canadian Mounted Police
recce	Reconnaissance
RMCC	Royal Military COllefe of Canada
RoCK	Representative of Canada in Kandahar
ROE	Rules of Engagement
SEAL	Sea-Air-Land
SF	Special Forces
SFA	Security Force Assistance
SME	Subject matter expert
SOC Africa	US Special Operations Command – Africa
SOCSOUTH	Special Operations Command (South)
SOUTHCOM	U.S. Southern Command
SOF	Special Operations Forces
SOPs	Standard Operating Procedures
SOTF	Special Operations Task Force
SWAT	Special Weapons and Tactics
TF	Task Force
TTPs	Tactics, Techniques and Procedures
UN	United Nations
US	United States

GLOSSARY

USSF	United States Special Forces
USSOCOM	United States Special Operations Command
UW	Unconventional Warfare
VSO	Village Stability Operations

INDEX

I N D E X

INDEX

INDEX